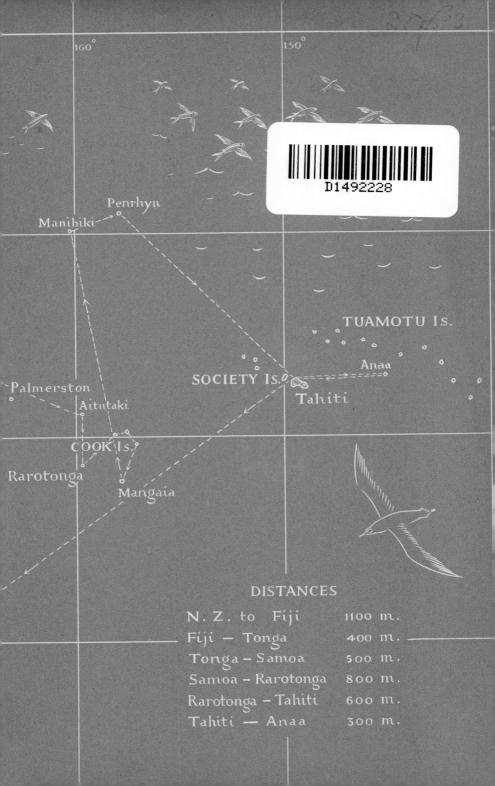

160°   150°

Penrhyn
Manihiki

TUAMOTU Is.

Anaa

SOCIETY Is.
Tahiti

Palmerston
Aitutaki

COOK Is.

Rarotonga

Mangaia

DISTANCES

N. Z. to Fiji   1100 m.
Fiji — Tonga   400 m.
Tonga — Samoa   500 m.
Samoa — Rarotonga   800 m.
Rarotonga — Tahiti   600 m.
Tahiti — Anaa   300 m.

OVER THE REEFS

WITH ENGRAVINGS BY THE AUTHOR

OVER THE REEFS

by

ROBERT GIBBINGS

LONDON: J. M. DENT & SONS LTD.

For
My Daughters in England
VAHINE AND TIARE

CHAPTER ONE

'YOU SEE,' said the White Knight to Alice, 'it 's as well to be provided for *everything*. That 's the reason the horse has anklets round his feet.'

'But what are they for?' Alice asked in a tone of great curiosity.

'To guard against the bites of sharks,' the Knight replied.

On the deck of a cutter sailing from Nukualofa, I said to the Crown Prince of Tonga: 'What are they for, those broken coco-nut shells strung on a bent twig?'

'Oh,' he said, 'those are garlands for the sharks.'

'And those wreaths of flowers on the deck?' I asked.

'Necklaces. Sometimes the sharks prefer them.'

'And that rope with the noose?'

'Another necklace. But we don't say very much about that—not just yet. By the way,' he added, 'I hope your conscience is clear—I mean, I hope that you are at peace with every one, that you have had no quarrels. The sharks won't come if there is any ill will at home. It is *very* important that our consciences should be clear.'

Three islands in the Tonga group are noted for their shark fishers, Eua Iki, Moungaone, and Uiha, and it was to the first of these, lying a few miles to the east of Tonga-tabu, that we were now heading to pick up fishermen expert in the art. Shark fishing in these islands is a highly skilled and ritualistic pursuit. The fishermen must prepare, both physically and mentally, for the task in hand. Strict continence is enforced the night before they set out. None may leave unexpiated a wrong done to his chief, nor harbour unkind thoughts against a neighbour. If any have failed to observe these precepts the sharks will not come. And while the fishermen are away there must be no noise or gaiety in the village, nor any discord. Smoke from the oven may not pass through the house of the head fisherman. It is the duty of his wife to remain indoors. It is the duty of the villagers to prepare food against the fishermen's return and to keep them constantly in their thoughts.

One is reminded of the Esquimaux of Alaska who before setting out on whaling expeditions subject themselves to rigorous discipline. The harpooner in particular must inure himself to extremes of physical exertion and pain. While he is away his wife must do little work, make no noise of any kind in the house, and often fast until his return. Another parallel is to be found in Laos, in Siam, where an elephant hunter about to set out warns his wife that if she cuts her hair while he is absent the elephant will break its bindings, if she oils her body the elephant will slip through the cords that hold it. And, again, among the deer-hunting Indians of California it was imperative that the women left behind in the village should spend most of their time quietly, indoors; neither might the children romp, shout, or throw stones. If these rules were not

2

kept the deer would be unmanageable and break from the stockade.

The sun had set when the men from Eua Iki came aboard. Long banks of lavender clouds lay close to the horizon against a golden afterglow. Birds that had shone white as foam at noon were now dark ghostly shapes, lost and found against an indigo sea flecked with silver.

From the hatch where he was sitting the prince reached for his guitar. 'I forgot to say,' he said, 'don't throw

anything overboard as we go along. The sharks don't like it.' Then he began to play, and to sing, very softly, in Tongan, a song of his own composing, and one by one the crew joined with him in the singing.

The light was fading rapidly, the wind dropping. The cutter rose and fell. One lost all sense of being on a boat, of being anywhere, indeed, but in a universe of water and music and gentle soothing movement; a strange unreal universe bounded by no other dimensions than the evening and the morning.

The prince stopped singing. 'Sikaleti will tell you the story,' he said.

Sikaleti was one of the crew. His name is Tongan for cigarette. There is no special significance in the name— one has to be called something. In Tonga parents do not consider names for their children before those children are born. When the time comes they call the child by any idea that may be in their head at the moment. There is a man called Makasina, which is Tongan for magazine; there is another called Aisikalimi, which means ice-cream; and there are others, Fonokelafi, Sitalaite, Benesine, which mean, respectively, phonograph, starlight, benzine.

Sikaleti began his story. 'In the earlier days, long while ago, there lived a very old couple on east shore of Tonga-tabu. This very old couple had young daughter and her name was Hina. They loved fishing very much. That was why they live alongside shore. And they loved to go in their little canoe, by the current in many ways, and look for fish. One day they caught a little shark, but without killing it. They saved its life for Hina. So Hina was very pleased, and she took the little shark and she put it in a pool between the rocks, just close by where she live. And every day she go along with piece of meat for the little shark and she call out over the stream: "Hina! Hina! Here is your lovely meat. Come and take it. And here is your garland of flowers that I have made for you." Then the shark come along, very cheerful. It run very quickly and catch the meat. But if one day, or another day, the little shark not come, then Hina shake the beads of coco-nut shell in the water. She make the beads all for that, and they sound very loud in the water. And the little shark it love that sound and it come up quick to Hina.

'But after a while the little shark grow larger and larger, and one day it run away into the sea. Then, when Hina come and call to it, the shark not come. And Hina very sad. She cry and she cry, and she shake the beads, and she shout to the shark. But the shark not come any more. Then she cry out and she say: "Hina! Hina! Come back! Come back and I will go with you." Then the

4

shark come back, and it take Hina and they go far away in the deep rough sea.

'So Hina's parents very sad, and they take their little canoe and they try follow the way Hina and the shark went on. They took some meat and a garland of perfumery flowers and beads of coco-nut shell too, and they cry out all the time and shake the beads in the water. And then Hina come up all of a sudden quick, and she have many sharks with her and she talk with the old couple. But she say she not go back with them, she say she not ride in canoe, she say she stay with the sharks. So old couple very sad and they start ride back home in their little canoe, and they take along with them the coco-nut beads and the garland of perfumery flowers and the meat.

'But Hina and the sharks wish very much to get those things. So they run very fast after the canoe, and Hina call out to the old couple and she say: "I not come back home, but you give me those three things." Then the old couple give Hina the garland and the beads and the meat. And they very sad, they mourn very much that she not come back. So Hina say to them: "All times when you want see me you come out into big ocean, and you shake beads, and you bring perfumery flowers, and you call, and then I come see you." And that is the end of the story.'

Tui Hakau, the head fisherman, now announced that fishing was about to begin.

The sea was oily calm, the wind had dropped completely. Sails flapped, ropes creaked. Four men were sitting, two on each side of the deck, with their legs over the side, their feet touching the water. Each of them held one of the coco-nut 'rattles,' the beads of Sikaleti's story. Tui Hakau stood on the deck holding a long pole at the far end of which was tied a lump of meat. He began to chant, and as he did so the men with the coco-nut rattles began to work them vigorously up and down in the water, churning it into a foam on both sides of the cutter. The sound produced was like that of a shoal of small fish breaking on the surface. And as Tui Hakau called into the mirrored darkness each phrase was echoed by the men on board; and as they chanted the prince translated to me.

'Come up! Come up from the deep!
Come, all you *neiufis*,
Come, all you *ahos*,
Come also, *kapakauhinganos* (species of shark).
Rise to the surface;
Come on board our boat
And wear the flower-wreaths that we have brought
    for you.
Hina, here is your garland!
Hina, here is your pillow!
Come to us, so that our waiting is worth while,
So that the music of our rattles is rewarded,
So that our incantations bear fruit.
Awake! all who are asleep.
Awake! and come to us.
Come up close and take the food that we offer you.
Hina, come, and let us make happiness together.
Hina, we are waiting for you.'

Almost every one on board was now making as much noise as possible. One was beating out a rhythm with two sticks, another was stamping a measure. The prince, having finished the translation for me, took up a heavy spar and thumped the deck. And all the while the chorus continued:

'Hina! Hina! Come up! Come up!'

But there was no sign of Hina.

The rope with its noose lay ready on the deck. It had been rove through the scupper so that once over the shark's head and hauled tight the animal could be held firmly against the side of the ship and quickly dispatched by a blow on the head with a club. 'Incidentally,' said the prince, 'if the man wielding the club should by any mis-chance drop it into the water, he is in honour bound to dive into the water and retrieve it, no matter how many sharks are about.' At this moment one of the crew

6

jumped overboard and began to swim and splash and dive in the wake of the ship. 'That will encourage the sharks,' said the prince. 'Sometimes they are shy.'

The swimmer climbed on board again and resumed his work with the rattle. 'If sharks should come around but not close enough to noose them,' said the prince, 'it is not unusual for a man to go overboard, swim out to them, and lead them in. I have seen men swimming shoulder to shoulder with the sharks, leading them to the bait. No!' he emphasized, in reply to a question of mine, 'no man of Eua Iki has ever been touched by a shark.'

The night wore on. The headsails were aback, the mainsail close-hauled. We were scarcely moving. And all the time the calling went on:

'Hina! Hina! Come up, come up!'

All thought was dominated by this chorus. There was no escape from it, one moment commanding, the next cajoling, pleading.

When any sea birds passed over or near us the words varied momentarily with exhortations to the birds to go and fetch their friends the sharks. Sea birds and sharks are thought to be friends because they often feed on the same shoal of fish, the sharks driving the fish up to the surface and the birds in their turn driving them down again to the sharks.

Close on midnight a last fragment of the moon broke through scudding cloud, and with it Hina, glistening with phosphorescent light, appeared beside us. Immediately there was silence. Only Tui Hakau might speak.

'Hina! Hina!' he said. 'Go back and fetch your friends. We want to see your friends.' He threw the garlands of flowers into the water. The trail of light disappeared.

'She will fetch her friends,' said the prince.

Every one was now watching, expectant, straining their eyes into the darkness. Sudden drenching showers of rain passed almost unnoticed.

7

Hina seemed to be away a long time. The only sound was the creaking and groaning of the tackle. The cutter lurched from side to side. One was vaguely conscious that the wind was rising.

Then the chorus began again:

'Hina, Hina, ko ho kakala 'e ni,
Hina, Hina, ko ho kali 'e ni,
Hina me'a mai ka e holo e lepa ni.'

With even more energy than before they shook the rattles. With even more energy than before they beat the deck. With even more energy they shouted.

But Hina did not come back.

Night turned to dawn, a grey dawn with the sun rising behind heavy clouds. After sunrise the wind increased. White crests broke on the passing waves. And still they called in vain.

Hina did not come back.

In rough weather sharks avoid the surface and, with the sudden change, she had gone with her friends into the deep waters. Yet a few days earlier those same fishermen had by the same method caught four sharks, and a few days later they caught fifteen. They say it is so simple to slip the noose over the shark's head when it comes for the bait.

CHAPTER TWO

THE BEST APPROACH to the Tongan islands is by plane. From that amazing dream-like world, where all below is cloud-flecked blue and overhead is only light, nebulae of islands appear and disappear. Each is like a sectioned agate. A central core of vivid green ringed with yellow sand—these in their turn encircled by the cool turquoise of the lagoon. And edging that, the surf on the reef, like a collar of white lace; and then the sapphire and amethyst of deep water.

From the air one can distinguish many varied coral formations. There are the single islets margined with pale waters. There are the wide mirror-like lagoons, whose surrounding reef is dotted with clusters of palms. There are islands that enclose lagoons and lagoons that hold islands. There are crescent peaks, craters of extinct volcanoes rising sheer from the sea. And there are shoals, veined as malachite, combed unceasingly by the ocean swell; and reefs, far below the surface, that will one day reach sea level.

Flying low over the larger islands one glimpses clusters of roofs, of mellow thatch or rusty iron, among the palms.

The foliage is too thick and the speed of the plane too great to discern much human activity inland, but here and there, by the shore or further out to sea, men may be seen fishing. On one shallow reach a man is casting his throw-net. On the next three men are building a fish trap. Near to another island two men in a launch are chasing a turtle.

The throw-net is in universal use among the people of Polynesia, as it would seem to be in most countries where

the temperature is high enough for fishermen to remain long in the water. In the Red Sea and Persian Gulf and along the shores of Africa, Ceylon, and China, it is in common use. The net is circular, about twelve feet in diameter, and weighted with small leads round its whole perimeter. In the shallow water of a lagoon, where shoals of small fish abound, a native moves stealthily, his net draped over one shoulder. Faint ripples or shadows in the waters, or faint reflections from the sea floor, betray the presence of a shoal. The net is thrown. It spreads to its widest and, as it strikes the water, the sinkers carry its edge quickly downward. The fisherman then draws it towards him, slowly, by the cord at its centre, and, as the weighted edge closes in, the fish are enmeshed.

Fish traps are infinitely varied. They may be weirs of stone or fences of coco-nut fronds, or, as is common to-day, screens of wire-netting kept in place by wooden stakes. They may be built across the mouth of a river or they may be constructed anywhere along the shallow coastal waters where fish come and go with the tides. The principle in all is the same—to guide the fish into small enclosures from which they are unlikely to escape. In Tonga a favourite pattern is 'the anchor,' the shaft of which is a long fence at right angles to the shore, and the flukes, the pockets on either side into which the fish are diverted. Near to where I lived in Nukualofa there was a trap, pentagonal in shape, and about seventy yards in

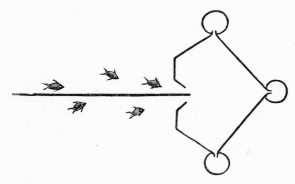

greatest diameter, into which the fish were guided by a weir; sometimes from one side, sometimes from another, according to the ebbing and flowing of the tide. The inner side of each wall led the fish to the circular enclosures whence, owing to the shape of the entrance, and because fish rarely make a sharp turn in their movements, it was difficult for them to find a way out.

Soon after my first arrival in Tongatabu I was invited to go turtle hunting. Tavita (David) and his brother Siaki (Jack) and I set out in a launch. Tavita is an all-the-year-round fisherman, seeking everything from whales to whitebait, in their seasons. When he hunts whales it is with the old-fashioned harpoon thrown from an open boat. Now that we were about to chase turtles our only equipment was a two-pronged spear with a ten-foot wooden handle.

It was a clear bright day, only a freckle of cloud, when

we set out for an island, about twelve miles to the north, where on the lee side the water would be shallow and crystal clear. Sail and engine carried us along merrily and, as we went, Tavita told me about two whales that he had killed in one day, a few months earlier. 'I take one of those whales along to the queen,' he said, 'and she tie him up on beach right beside palace. And the other whale I fetch him up on shore close by my house where I live, and I cut him up and I sell him for meat to the folks. Folks mighty glad buy whale meat because whale meat same thing like shark meat, he keep much longer than beef meat. Oh, I sell pounds and pounds and pounds. Folks come back second time, and they say: "Tavi, you let me have some more of that whale." Then policeman come along, and he say: "Tavi, your whale stink." And I say: "My whale not stink, my whale pretty good beef." He say: "Tavi, your whale rotten; he stink bad. You take him away out in deep sea; let sharks have him." So I say: "What about queen's whale? You been along to queen, say her whale stink?" And he say: "Queen's whale not stink, only your whale stink." And I say: "That damn funny." And he say: "Yes, damn funny." And I say: "Damn funny, but nothing for a laugh." And he say: "I guess you right." Then we both laugh. After that he come along with me and we fetch whale out into deep sea and we leave him there for sharks.'

On reaching the fishing-grounds we had scarcely got our sails down when, among the patterns on the sea floor, a turtle was seen. It needs a trained eye to distinguish one patch of purple that is potentially mobile from another that is essentially immobile, but the eyes of Siaki and Tavita had had that training. The chase was on. Tavita, almost naked, stood in the bow, holding the spear. Siaki was at the helm, obeying every sign and word of his brother. The tactics were to outflank the turtle and drive it towards the shore. Only when forced to the surface for air would it offer an opportunity for the spear, only in shallow water could a diver hope to grapple with it. The launch swung here, swung there, speeding for a few moments and then slowing again, swerving sharply as the quarry changed direction, overrunning it as it doubled back. It seemed to be a question of which could best combine speed with stratagem.

But after a while the turtle began to tire. Its movements grew slower. It seemed to be swimming nearer to the surface. Then for a moment its head shot from the water, and as suddenly it sank again. Now the creature was moving with renewed energy—it was surprising that in such a short space of time an animal could take in so much air. Again we were speeding and, as we did so, Tavita, lifting himself on tiptoe on the deck, thrust with all his might. But the water was too deep and the spear came back to the surface with one prong bent, showing that it had touched the tough carapace. Goaded by the blow, the turtle spurted again, but the effort was of short duration. Now we were in shallower water. Tavita discarded the spear and stood ready to plunge. Of a sudden he was in the water and almost as suddenly he was at the surface again, with the struggling animal in his arms. He had clasped it from behind with an arm under each fore-flipper and one hand pressing down the head. The hunt was over.

Three more turtles were sighted and each one was chased, but without success. Then with the falling tide there were no more elusive shadows in the water. The turtles had gone out to sea.

The old chief, Tui Malila, once looked Captain Cook in the face. It was, indeed, Captain Cook who brought him to Tonga in 1777. Tui Malila is now old and his sight is dim. He is not a hereditary chief; it is because of his great age and dignity that the title was conferred upon him. Because, too, of that age and dignity he has been given apartments in the royal palace. When the royal kava ring is formed he takes his place, in due order of precedence, and is served with his cup.

Because of his age and infirmity he travelled in a royal car when he came to sit to me for his portrait. Perhaps sit isn't quite the right word; he didn't like remaining still. In spite of all requests he would insist on moving about the lawn, sniffing the flowers, sometimes plucking them, plucking even the buds, and at times the young shoots. But then he is old, and he has suffered much in his time. On one occasion he was overtaken by a bush fire and almost burned to death, but, tumbling into a hole in the ground, he lay there, sheltered by smouldering branches, until the danger was past. After that he did not leave the palace grounds for a long while. When he did, while wandering alone, he was kicked by a horse—the mark on his side is still to be seen. But he is apparently happy. Although for the most part sedentary in his habits he does, occasionally, go for quite long rambles. If he were not a tortoise it would all be very strange.

CHAPTER THREE

NOMUKA, in the Haapai group of Tonga, was the last island that Captain Bligh visited as commander of the *Bounty*. The ship had left that island but a few hours, and was running before a light easterly breeze in the direction of Tofua, when the mutiny broke out.

I sailed in those same waters. Nomuka, to the south-east, showed as a line of palms on the horizon. Tofua, to the north-west, stood higher and more austere, a rocky plateau. Near to it the cone of Kao rose into its ever-present nimbus of cloud. In Tongan, the word *kao* means cloud. Many a high island, still below the horizon, may be located by the stationary cloud which hovers over it; many an unseen atoll may be found by the light reflected from its lagoon.

On the schooner on which we were travelling men and women sat or lay in all directions, among bundles of mats and tapa cloth, brightly coloured wooden boxes and woven baskets. Naked children sprawled on the deck. On one side of the cabin skylight a mother and her two children were curled amid baskets of fruit and coco-nuts, loaves of bread, an umbrella, a bar of soap, and a jar of water. Beyond this group, eight men and two women were stretched on the deck, feet towards the rail. On the bridge at the wheel stood a splendid young native—a direct descendant of an Archbishop of York, I was told, however he managed it. For'ard, again, one could discern the hindquarters of a cow. In a lifeboat swung over the side the ship's cook was dozing, his hand on a fishing-line tied to a thwart of the boat. Close by on the deck lay three large fish, streamlined ingots of silver.

The smouldering fires of the volcano, still active on Tofua, were faintly visible from the ship. This is an opening to Pulotu, the underworld, I was told. When any one dies in the Haapai islands, singing or crying is heard within the volcano. If it is singing it indicates that the soul is happy, its conscience free; but if it is crying that is heard, the augury is not so favourable.

Some fifteen miles to the north of Nomuka lies the island of Tongua, and here it was that once upon a time there lived a certain chief and his family. One day the daughter of this chief became very ill. Nothing that he or her mother could do for her was of any help, and nothing that the wise men of the island could do for her brought the least improvement. She just got worse and worse, until everybody feared that she was going to die.

So, in despair, the chief sent off two messengers in a canoe to Fiji, in search of someone who might effect a cure. They sailed at dawn, and all that day and throughout the next day the wind helped them, but they were at sea many days and many nights before they reached the island of Moala in the Lau group, which lies to the south-east of Fiji.

It was night-time when they landed and very dark, and there were no lights in the houses because all the people had gone fishing. On all the island they could see only one small light, and that was close to the shore, and when they got to it they found that it came from a very small house, a little *fale* no bigger than a cookhouse. And because it was so small they hesitated to go in. But they knocked, and a voice answered: 'Come in.' Then they looked through the door and there was no one inside. The little house was empty. There were no mats, no food bowls—the only thing they could see was a basket hanging from the rafters. So they knocked a second time, and again a voice said to them: 'Come in.' So they went in; but there was nobody there. Then they went outside and they knocked again, and a third time they heard a voice saying to them: 'Come in.' So they went in again, and this time the voice said to them: 'What is it you want? Tell me what it is you want.' And the voice came from inside the basket, and when they looked inside the basket there was a man's skull.

16

'What is it you want?' said the skull. 'Tell me what it is you want.'

Then they told the skull the reason of their coming.

'Take me with you,' said the skull. 'Return to your island and take me with you. I will cure her.'

So they set out again in the canoe, taking the skull with them, and they rowed with their paddles for many days and many nights until at last, late one evening, they saw their island. But as they approached they could see torches being lit all around the chief's house, and they were very sad because that meant that the chief's daughter was dead.

'Hurry! Hurry!' said the skull. 'Her spirit has not yet left her body.'

Then they worked harder than ever with their paddles, and when they reached land they carried the skull up to the chief's house and they put it under the tapa cloth which in Tonga is spread over a dead person. That is what the skull had told them to do. And, very soon, the daughter of the chief began to stir under the tapa cloth, and soon after that she sat up, and in a little while she was quite recovered and brought back to life.

'Take me back to Moala,' said the skull.

So the two men put the skull into the basket and took it down to the canoe. But the chief called out to them. 'Who did you bring to cure my daughter?' he said. 'Where is he?'

Then the two men went back to the chief and they told him that it was the skull that had cured his daughter.

'It is a pity,' said the chief, 'that it wasn't a living man, for then he should have had my daughter for his wife.'

With that the two men returned to their canoe and were about to set out once more when the skull spoke again.

'What did the chief say?' asked the skull.

So the two men told what he had said.

'Take me out,' said the skull, 'to where the waves are breaking white on the reef, and throw me into the deep water.'

The men obeyed his command. They paddled across the

lagoon and threw the basket with its contents into the deep water beyond the reef. Hardly had they done so than there came from the sea, shooting the white foam of the breakers, a young man of outstanding beauty. And as they watched they saw him swim ashore and go straight to the chief's house. Before they themselves reached land they heard the sounds of merriment from within.

The daughter was given in marriage and, from that day to this, any man of Moala who comes to Tongua is given a royal welcome. Whatsoever he desires is given to him; whatsoever he may wish to do is permitted. And should a man of Tongua visit Moala he is greeted in the same way. And this was told to me by the high chief of Tongua as we travelled on the schooner *Hifofua* from Nukualofa to Lifuka.

This idea of regeneration through immersion was one that I met with again and again throughout the Islands. It has, of course, its parallels in the Christian belief in baptism, and in the healing powers attributed to sacred rivers, such as the Jordan and Ganges, but these do not concern us here. On Samoa I heard a legend in which a man, so small and ill-favoured that he was compelled to live as an outcast from his village, plunged into a spring, and after remaining awhile in its depths returned to the surface, healed of his infirmities and grown to heroic stature. In Rarotonga, in the Cook Islands, I was shown where an ancient well had but recently been filled in. It is still believed that in that well it was possible for priests of the old religion to drown people afflicted with leprosy and bring them back to life cleansed of their infirmity. About the year 1824 Te-uira-a-Tangaloa, 'the first king of the Evangelical time,' who was covered with scars and sores, was put to death in this manner and restored to life completely cured. On Rurutu, in the Austral Isles, 'there was a chief called Toromana who had leprosy put on him. He was thrown into a well called Teoaa and brought out again clean.'

On all sides, from the deck of the schooner, one saw islands and islets, many of them scarce higher than their tallest trees. If we had been sailing a few years earlier we might have sighted Falcon Island, thirty-five miles to the west of Nomuka. But to-day its highest point is below sea level. Its foundation is a submarine volcano and because of that its aspect, not to mention its appearance and disappearance, varies considerably from year to year. When first sighted by H.M.S. *Falcon* in 1865 it was hardly more than a shoal, but since then successive eruptions have caused it to 'rise and fall' so that it has become known as Jack-in-the-Box Island. Ashes and lava dust are unstable components in land formation, and hardly has the island come into being than it is weathered away. After one upheaval it stood nearly five hundred feet high and was over a mile in length, but within a few years wind and rain had again reduced it to sea level. In 1927, when its height was about three hundred and fifty feet, the Government of Tonga sent ambassadors to plant its flag and annex the island only to find, soon afterwards, that the new possession had disappeared beneath the waves.

In spite of the fact that Tasman, Cook, and Bligh watered their ships at Nomuka, there was nothing that I could see when I got there that suggested an illustration in any way distinctive of their landing place, such as I had hoped to make. The crescent bay where successive boats' crews had come ashore was edged with white sand and bounded by palms and evergreens. It might have been almost any bay on almost any tropic island.

'You must make a drawing, the place is historic,' said His Britannic Majesty's consul and agent, with whom I was travelling.

'But there's nothing to draw,' I said.

'The place is historic,' repeated the consul.

'Can't you hear the man muttering?' said Fred Wiseman, the third member of the party, referring to me. 'In basic language those grunts can mean nothing but negation.'

'Even an artist has his duties,' said the consul.

'If you would forget duties and diplomatic phraseology, and observe gestures and primitive articulation of sounds,' said Wiseman, 'you would infer that the landscape is not suitable for expression through the medium of wood-engraving, that the mosquitoes are innumerable, that the artist got soaked in the last shower, that he thinks another shower is imminent, and that anyway he doesn't feel like drawing just now.'

'The trouble is,' I said, 'that great men about to perform great deeds seldom consider the artists who come after them. They appear to be entirely lacking in a sense of pictorial composition. The plain of Marathon was nothing but a plain, the field of Waterloo nothing but a field.'

'What about Wolfe who stormed the Heights of Abraham, and Rooke who took Gibraltar?' asked the consul.

'They were exceptions,' I said. 'Wolfe was a poet at heart, and Rooke must certainly have had something of an artist's blood in his veins for it was Noel Rooke, a relation of his, who taught me wood-engraving.'

'You see,' said the consul, 'how a man who is pre-occupied in his work may become utterly indifferent to the wider significance of historic events.'

'All the vowel sounds are very primitive,' said Wiseman, 'yet they appear to have retained their original meanings. Their use in response to emotion seems to be the same throughout mankind.'

'Oh!' said the consul, with emphasis, as if in distress.

'"Oh" and "ah" were expressions before ever there was organized language,' continued Wiseman. 'But whereas "Ah" is scarcely a word—in fact hardly more than a sigh —and at times non-committal in meaning, "Oh" is always the response to something exciting wonder. When a Fijian chief enters the *vale* the respectful natives squatting on the ground clap their hands three times, to show that they carry no weapons, while in unison they chant a long "Oh . . .! oh . . .! oh . . .!" It is a mark of very great respect.'

'"Oh, SOPHONISBA! SOPHONISBA, oh!"' quoted the consul, as we turned to retrace our steps.

CHAPTER FOUR

IF THERE WAS NOTHING compelling to the pencil at any of the historic places in the Haapai group of Tonga, it was different on the main island, Tongatabu. There, there was not only the impressive archway of coral rock, known as the Ha'amonga, but there were also many royal tombs of vast extent. So far no satisfactory explanation of the Ha'amonga has been found, but there is a pleasant tale, told by an aged Tongan, that it was erected in the eleventh century by one of the kings of Tonga who, fearing dissension in his family after his death, wished to impress upon his two sons the sacred bond of brotherhood. Each of the upright columns of the trilithon represents a son, while the massive lintel, morticed into its supports, typifies the bond which should exist between them.

The word *ha'amonga* in Tongan means a burden, as borne on a carrying stick, often on the shoulders of two men, and it is easy to suppose that the name of the monument arose from such a connection in the minds of the people. Tongans, like other Polynesians, are quick to appreciate shapes and patterns, and to call them by names which suggest a parallel. In Samoa the word *amonga* again signifies a burden, and there the word is used to indicate the constellation we know as Orion's Belt; the two outer stars representing the baskets at either end of a carrying pole, the centre star being the head of the carrier. In a similar

way in Samoa the word *sumu* is applied not only to the Southern Cross but to a fish whose contour suggests the four stars. In Samoa, too, the Great Bear becomes, more reasonably, *Anava*, the War Club; the Pleiades are called *Li'i*, a word which signifies either a crop of seedlings or a rash on the body.

More than forty of the royal tombs, called *langi*, are found in the Tongan group, the majority being in or near the village of Mua, the former royal capital. These *langi*, whose name also means the sky—the vault of heaven—are immense truncated and terraced pyramids, rectangular in plan. At their base they measure as much as a hundred and fifty feet in length and breadth. In as many as five terraces, they may rise to a height of twelve feet, and individual stones are found up to eighteen feet in length, of several feet in thickness, and standing chest-high from the ground. Under the upper terrace are one or more stone-lined vaults in which several of the same family may be buried. It is told of the *langi* at Fangaloto—meaning deep anchorage—that once, when the mutilated body of a murdered king was washed ashore, an attendant at the court, conceiving it beneath the dignity of the king to be buried without a head, had his own head removed and

buried with the royal torso. Other stories suggest that this act of devotion was not exceptional. There is an expression, 'Hibiscus to hibiscus,' which was used on such occasions if the willing victim was of high rank. The hibiscus-tree has a particularly tough bark often utilized as cord: only other hibiscus is of equal strength. The phrase is used to-day when a strong and capable man is succeeded by one of equal strength and capability. But if a man of vigorous character is succeeded by a weaker one, it is said that 'banana has been added to hibiscus'—the banana stem being loose-fibred and brittle.

The stepped pyramid is found again and again throughout Polynesia, sometimes as a tomb, sometimes as the altar
of a *marae*. In the Papara district of Tahiti there is a
mound overgrown with trees that marks where a shrine
once stood. It was built about the year 1768, and measured
ninety yards in length and thirty yards in width, with eleven
steps reaching to a height of fifty feet from the ground. Of
recent origin, the tomb of Queen Marau, whom I remember
as a mighty stately figure, measures twenty feet in length
and six feet in width, with six terraces built of pebbles set
in cement. Perhaps the most notable exception to this
general design is in Tahiti also, where, at his own request,
the memorial to Pomare V, the last reigning monarch of
the island, is in the form of a tower whose summit is
crowned with the model of a benedictine bottle. He had
a special liking for the liqueur, and indeed there were times
when he may well have needed some little drop of comfort.
It was he who, when discussing the possibility of a suc-
cessor to his throne, said: 'The queen has children, I have
none.'

On the other hand, it is possible that his taste for cordials
was hereditary. His ancestor, Pomare II, also had 'a
leaning and a liking' that way. In a letter to one Hassall
in Sydney, dated 1st January 1807, he wrote: 'Sir, I shall
esteem it a favour if you can procure me a Still in return
for which, if hogs be acceptable, please write to me that
I may know how many.'

That same Pomare II, who died in 1821, was the first
king of Tahiti to accept Christianity, a move on his part
not without political advantage. Nor as time went on did
he forget the perquisites that might be attendant on con-
version. In one of his many letters to the London
Missionary Society, we find: 'Friends, I hope you also
will consent to my request which is this: I wish you to
send a great number of men, women, and children here.
Friends, send also property and cloth for us. Friends,
send also plenty of musquettes and powder, for wars are
frequent in our country. This also I wish, that you would

send me all the curious things you have in England. Also send me everything necessary for writing: Paper, Ink, and Pens in abundance; let no writing utensil be wanting. Friends, I have done, and have nothing at all more to ask you for.'

CHAPTER FIVE

From TONGA TO SAMOA. Three quiet days at sea with dawns and flying fish and sunsets for company. Whereas nowhere on Tongatabu, the main island of the Tongan group, is the land more than three hundred feet high, and among the outlying islands only a few isolated peaks reach higher, on all sides of Upolu the land rises from a low coastal belt to form a mountainous core, with peaks averaging a height of between two and three thousand feet, and Mount Fito, its highest point, three thousand six hundred feet above the sea. These bush-clad hills form the background to Apia, the capital, whose low white buildings encircle the harbour. Tongatabu, Vavau, and most of the Tongan archipelago of over a hundred and fifty islands, are entirely of coral; Upolu and Savai'i, the two principal islands of Western Samoa, are volcanic in origin—one peak of Savai'i is about five thousand feet above sea level. Dominating Apia is Mount Vaea, where, on the summit, is the tomb of Robert Louis Stevenson. To reach that summit is a big climb. I did not make it because I could see no advantage accruing to any one else if I did so, and considerable disadvantage accruing to me. It was the beginning of the hot season when I reached the island and, by all accounts, an exceptionally hot beginning. It was impossible to put on, let alone wear, a dry shirt. The mere effort of changing the garments made one pour with sweat.

It came as no small surprise to me to find, almost within a few hours of my going ashore, that I was addressed as 'Tusitala.' But then I learned that the word is not a title; it means no more than author, a teller of tales: *tusi*, to write; *tala*, a story.

I had landed at Apia less than a week before that all-important event on the island, the rising of the *palolo*. Twice only in the year, and then for but an hour or less, these worms emerge in myriads from the crevices in the coral and wriggle to the surface of the lagoon, there, male and female, to complete the cycle of their lives. To the Samoan they are a special delicacy and, when the state of the moon indicates that the rise is imminent, great preparations for their capture take place along the coast, and long journeys are made to those parts of the island where they are most likely to appear.

But before I could undertake any expedition it was necessary to find an interpreter. There was no trouble about that. Charlie Olsen turned up and appointed himself. Of middle age and mixed parentage, he had spent most of his life in the Islands, at one time supercargo on a schooner, later running a trading store on some out-of-the-way island. Now he was waiting to get a passage on a ship going to the Cook Islands and, meanwhile, he offered his services.

So one afternoon a few days later we set out, in hopes of seeing the *palolo* rise. Charlie had brought with him, for me, a 'talking chief,' or orator, who he said was a necessity on such occasions. All the portents favoured '*palolo* weather.' Prophets foretold heavy rain before the following dawn. Although the sky was clear overhead, tall towers of cloud stretched up angrily from the horizon. The day was oppressively hot. There had even been a mild earthquake.

For the first twenty miles we journeyed by car, a means of travel all too rapid for one but recently arrived in Samoa and wishful to see the landscape. The road followed the coast. Through village after village we passed, each one orderly and trim. The thatched dwellings open on all sides might, save for their larger size, have been summer-houses in an English garden; the wide lawns, shaded by

spreading trees and accented with flowering shrubs, completed the illusion.

Inland, behind the villages, one glimpsed a blue tapestry of palm-covered hills. To seaward children were splashing in the shallows. In the deeper water of the lagoon men were fishing from canoes. In clear spring wash-pools, close beside the road, women, bare to the waist, were pounding clothes. We saw men carrying baskets of coco-nuts and bunches of bananas on poles; women carrying bundles of sugar-cane leaves on their shoulders; and small naked children with smaller naked children on their backs. We passed through plantations of coco-nuts, of bananas, of taro. There were horses tethered under the palm-trees, there were pigs untethered on the road. At almost every mile a village, at almost every half-mile a church: churches like barns, churches like pagodas, churches baroque, churches rococo, all built of cement and tin—vast tabernacles of incongruity. On the lawns freshly made bark cloth was spread to dry; copra, too, shining white, and cocoa beans like golden pebbles glittering in the sun. And everywhere the sparkle of flowers in sunshine: scarlet of hibiscus and poinsettias, purple of bougainvillea, yellow of candle flowers, ivory of frangipane, and crimson of wild ginger.

All the time I was impressed not only by the superb physique of the men and women whom we passed but with the grace and dignity of their carriage. Unhurried, with heads held high, they moved along the road with the ease and lightness of dancers. Nowhere else had I seen, nor outside of Samoa did I afterwards come across, anything to approach the simple loveliness in face and form and movement of these amber-skinned people. Their dress, too, had a classic comeliness; the men with torsos bare, girded about the loins with a *lavalava* reaching to the ankle; the women with flared bell-like dresses over the longer *lavalavas*, enclosing them as the outer petals encircle the inner petals of a double flower; young girls with the *lavalava* only, falling from breast to knee or crossing the breasts to tie behind the neck.

When the road became scarcely more than a track we left the car and continued our journey on foot. The villages became fewer and the landscape less tutored. Our path wound among palms. Sometimes their tall slender stems would tell dark against the sky; at other times they would shine silver, tinged with russet lichens, against a dense background of evergreen foliage. One was conscious of broad leaves, shining and spatulate, springing from the ground; of trailing creepers hanging in lace-like curtains from the tallest trees; of light filtering through a canopy of tremulous fronds. Arches of gnarled roots and fern-covered branches framed glimpses of dazzling sand and water. A sudden rain squall momentarily hid the nearby island of Manono.

The track grew narrower, the bush more dense. We travelled in single file. Glints of sunlight lit the harlequin wings of butterflies. Carmine-breasted birds dipped their

long bills into scarlet flowers. Birds, flashed with gold, hovered among yellow blossoms. A kingfisher, the *tiotala*, bright as in England, flew across our track. In the past such an omen would have deterred an army from going further. But when a small bronze lizard showed itself on the path and ran ahead of us for a few yards, I was assured that all was well. It would offset the kingfisher; we could now continue our course without anxiety.

At each village a chief came from his house to greet us. Would we not come in and rest awhile? Would we not drink kava? Many a time I would have liked to do so, but time was getting on; indeed, it had got on—the light was already fading. Crickets began their scythe-sharpening clamour. Flying foxes took wing. In places the ground became swampy; elsewhere the track was almost hidden by undergrowth. In the gathering darkness we slipped on fallen coco-nut fronds and stumbled over fallen tree-trunks. It was quite dark when we emerged on to a wide stretch of sand that flanked an estuary. But ahead of us we could see the lights of our destination twinkling, and canoes were waiting to ferry us to the village.

On arrival we were taken to the guest house, an oval Samoan *fale* of posts supporting a domed roof of thatch, raised on a platform of large stones. The posts had been decorated with plaited palm fronds, and inside were festoons of flowers and ferns. On the white coral floor mats had been laid, otherwise there were no furnishings. I was led to the place of honour at one end, where I sat down cross-legged with Charlie and my orator, one on either side of me. Almost immediately chiefs began to arrive. They came forward and shook hands, laying dried kava roots, symbols of friendship, before me. Then each sat down, taking his place, according to rank, beside one of the house posts, the high chief facing me from the opposite end of the building. Outside it was dark and silent. Inside the light was dim, but there was sufficient to show the features and bare shoulders of the men who sat there with such dignity.

An orator began to speak.

'Grateful thanks to Almighty God and King George Sixth that they confer with your excellency Lopati Kipingi (Samoan for my name), the distinguished writer from Peritania (Britain), to accomplish this journey. To-day is a very beautiful day. We are met in the time of evening, but I should call it also the time of morning because our expectation is fulfilled and you arrive. The sky is swept of clouds. As David say, it is a thing beautiful to behold, the coming together of brothers. Thanks very much to Almighty God that you arrive safely, that we meet in good of health, in very good of humour, and of a splendid evening.' My interpreter stopped speaking, and the orator continued his speech.

Oratory and ceremony play an important part in Samoan life, not least in the etiquette of travel. No chief goes on a journey unaccompanied by his orator, whose primary duty it is to make the frequent speeches that custom demands. This 'talking chief' must be familiar with the courtly language used when addressing men of rank, and with the special titles connected with each village through which their journey takes them. Formal speech is a highly developed art in Samoa, and possibly in no other country is a greater value set upon felicity of phrase or subtle play on words. They have sayings: 'The young of birds are fed on fish, but the young of men are fed with words'; 'Stones wear away, but not words.'

While the speech continued—and there was much of it, including a parable of David and Goliath in which I was likened to the young man who 'fetched a rolling stone from the running water and put it in his suit-case,' afterwards using it to slay the giant, as I was about to slay all untruth concerning Samoa—I could hear the sound of pounding near by, and, in the flare of a coconut-leaf torch, I caught a glimpse of a young man busy with stone pestle and mortar. This was the first stage in the preparation of the kava; the next was the arrival of the *taupou*, the ceremonial maiden of the village, who slipped quietly into the *fale* and took her place on the floor behind the wooden kava bowl that was in readiness awaiting her. Then the young man who had been active with the pestle carried in the pounded kava root, in a bread-fruit leaf, and tipped it into the empty bowl. Having done so he sat down on the right of the girl, and with the half-shell of a coco-nut ladled water into the bowl. Meanwhile the *taupou* had held out her hands to be rinsed by an attendant on her left. Then, dreamily, she settled herself behind the bowl, almost as a bird settles itself on its nest; dreamily she took a wisp of bast, and, with a curiously abstracted air, began to mix the grey fibrous particles of the kava root with the water. As if in a trance, her hands moved slowly and rhythmically, kneading and sieving the contents of the bowl. Then she lifted the bast high above the bowl, wringing it, and of a sudden she had thrown it behind her. It was caught by a youth who had been waiting, outside, in readiness. With whip-like movements he cracked it from side to side, jerking the fragments of kava root from its tissues. Then he threw it back to the girl. Again and again the kava was strained through the fibre; again and again the fibre was thrown to be cleansed. Mixing and sieving, wiping the rim of the bowl, then sieving again, silently the process went on.

The orator's voice, low-toned at first, was now loud and resounding. He had worked himself into a frenzy of final grandiose declamation. As he concluded, general murmurs of approbation greeted his peroration. Charlie translated, but modestly I will quote only his final words: 'Let us now drink the cup of Tusitala, Sovereign Lord of the Pacific, who by his writing rules the world.'

Another orator then announced that the kava was ready, clapping his hands as he spoke. Everybody else clapped also. Then a youth clad only in a *lavalava* rose to his feet and, filling a polished coco-nut shell from the kava bowl, raised it above his head and stood awaiting the orator's instructions. In a loud, high-pitched intonation the title of the first recipient was called, and in the phrase I heard the word Tusitala. The cup-bearer approached and, stooping before me, presented the cup. Taking it from him, I poured a few drops on to the floor as a libation to the ancient gods; then, saluting the assembled company with the word 'Manuia,' I drank the contents. The high chief sitting opposite to me next received the cup, and after him it was Charlie's turn; then the chief next in seniority, then our orator, and so, alternately between guests and hosts, until all of title had been served.

Many times after this in Samoa I was to drink kava with similar ceremony, for kava drinking never takes place without its elaborate ritual. No undertaking of any importance can be initiated without its use. As Sir Peter Buck has written, 'kava is the universal medium of hospitality. It corresponds to the tea, coffee, and alcohol of higher cultures as a means to ordinary social intercourse, and it forms the introduction to all ceremonies and matters of great pitch and moment.'

The Rev. George Turner, one of the early missionaries, tells us that in the olden times 'the head of the family, in taking his cup of *'ava* at the commencement of the evening meal, would pour out a little of it on the ground, as a drink-offering to the gods, and, all being silent, he would utter aloud the following prayer:

'"Here is *'ava* for you, O gods! Look kindly towards this family; let it prosper and increase; and let us all be kept in health. Let our plantations be productive; let fruit grow; and may there be abundance of food for us, your creatures.

'"Here is *'ava* for you, our war gods! Let there be a strong and numerous people for you in this land.

'"Here is *'ava* for you, O sailing gods! Do not come on shore at this place; but be pleased to depart along the ocean to some other land."'

In appearance the muddiness of the liquid is not attractive, but in flavour it has a pleasant peppery astringency. I know of no drink more refreshing when one is hot and tired after a long walk in the sun. Contrary to the statements of men zealous in repression, it is *not* intoxicating. Excessive use may have a temporary effect on the legs but not on the head.

The moon in its last quarter showed faintly through breaks in rainfull clouds when, between three and four o'clock next morning, we picked our way to the shore and climbed into the long-boat that awaited us. Most of the villagers had already set out in canoes, and we could see an occasional light flickering from them, far out on the lagoon. With quick, short strokes of the oars we moved across the dark bay, sensing rather than seeing the rowers on the thwarts. A tall figure, with a pole in his hands, showed faintly in the bow as he warded us from the widespread 'nigger-heads' of coral. The water was ankle-deep

in the bottom of the boat; the bursting of a cloud above
our heads added another inch to its depth.

We could hear the plashing of paddles in the water.
Greetings were called by people whom we could not see.
When a faint light crept into the sky, passing canoes
appeared as ghostly silhouettes. The sound of the surf
breaking on the reef came to us like the muffled roar of a
distant city. From time to time torches were flashed into
the water, water that shone iridescent, crystalline, with
coral in domes and cupolas, in hummocks, spurs, and
ledges, colourful as semi-precious stones. When I was in
the Red Sea and, equally, when I was in the West Indies,
I thought that the coral there was more splendid than any
to be found elsewhere; but when I returned to the Pacific
I knew that nothing could compare with the reefs that I
saw below me. The love of the moment seems the love
of all time—at the moment.

As no *palolo* had appeared a discussion arose as to whether
it might not be the wrong day of the year, but when the

prediction of a certain elderly chief was mentioned all doubts were removed. Another shower broke over us— I might have said another ocean enveloped us. Then of a sudden the word was passed: *palolo* had been seen. Immediately dip nets of muslin were swept through the water. Here a worm was caught; there, another; then they came in scores. The excitement grew intense. Soon they were appearing in thousands. The sea was alive with wriggling green and gold threads, knotted and twisted as wet twine gets twisted, but always wildly alive, rushing here, hurrying there, madly purposeful as bees in swarm. Every one was busy with scoop nets, ladling the harvest into sacks and baskets. Men and women leapt overboard into the shallow water, the better to sweep the sea. The baskets were filling quickly, and the captured worms, with the eggs which they had extruded, seethed in a slimy mass. Then came another shower, and after that a sudden calm —a calm not only above but below the water. The rise was over.

From behind the hills the sun shot forth its light; beyond the reef a milk-grey horizon foreshadowed further rain. All the canoes were heading homewards. Thoughts of dry clothes and food came uppermost in my mind.

For some delicacies a taste must be acquired, others need disguise before they can be appreciated. At breakfast Charlie and I were joined by a half-European trader who had also been on the expedition. We were served with fried eggs and spinach.

'Curious taste, this spinach,' I said. 'It's got a flavour of oysters.'

'Spinach be damned,' said the trader. 'That's *palolo*; better than any oysters. Though there's some,' he added as he scraped his plate, 'who think it smells like the reef at low tide.'

CHAPTER SIX

A FEW DAYS LATER, outside the post office at Apia, I met the trader with whom I had breakfasted after the *palolo* fishing. His name escaped my memory, so I had to ask him for it again.

'Stanton,' he said, showing me an envelope that was in his hand. 'There you are, H. E. Stanton, Esq., Henry Egerton Stanton. Henry after Henry VII, but you call me Harry. Every one calls me Harry.'

'Why Henry VII?' I asked.

'You come along to my house one day and I'll show you. No, you come along with me now, in the bus. You got nothing to do. You write, don't you? Well, you got nothing to do. You come along now. Only a few miles along the road.'

So we strolled together over the wooden bridge that crosses the Vaisingano River, and past the big white cathedral, to the Gold Star Garage. 'Yes,' he said, 'I got plenty you'd like to see. Oh, I got tons of stuff—clubs, fish-hooks, all sorts of things. I got a few books, too, but I don't read; I don't hold with reading, though I reckon a good book now and again does no man any harm.'

We climbed into a bus crammed to overflowing with

human beings, and found seats on boxes, one on either side of a sack crammed to overflowing with a pig.

Harry was a big man with the strong features and the dark crisp hair of a Samoan; his skin was of a deeper colour than many of them, and there was little about him to suggest his part-European parentage except the grey colour of his eyes and his lurching walk. He had a slight droop in one eye and a corresponding droop in one corner of his mouth, a corner that always held a cigarette, lit or unlit. The old khaki trousers that he had worn when after *palolo* had been replaced by a newer pair of the same colour, for town wear, and the faded blue shirt that he now wore was rather less faded than the one in which I had seen him at our first meeting. He had on his head a wide-brimmed straw hat, with elaborate coloured patterns woven into the crown. The brim, like the rest of it, showed signs of age—in one place a split in the weaving had been mended with a piece of sticking-plaster above and below.

In that seething crush of hot humanity it seemed a long while before the bus started. As we waited, Harry pointed out a house with a rusty iron roof on the far side of the bay. 'That's Tina McCrory's,' he said. 'That's the place for you to stay. You go along and see if she has a room. Yes, I know what you told me—that place where you stay now is no good to you. You want somewhere quiet, with a bit of good food. Tina will fix you. Tell her King Harry sent you—she always calls me King Harry.'

At last the bus jolted out of the garage yard. Away we went, picking up more and, incredibly, still more passengers and parcels at each corner of the town. Harry would keep making me turn round in my cramped position to see people or things behind my back.

'Look at that girl! Look at her, the one in shorts; look at her! No business to go about the streets like that. There's Charlie McPhee painting. A strong man on the theatre stage in Australia once, with muscles bulging like taro roots. Then he joined a dance band with an accordion, and then he came down here as a policeman. All of a sudden he becomes an artist, goes about the place with a paint-box. One day he's sitting in front of the cathedral, the next day he'll be painting a *fale* and a couple of palms. You'd pass it a hundred times, just a *fale* and a couple of palms; then Charlie comes along and makes a damn' nice picture of it. There's the Mau headquarters—you know: "Samoa for the Samoans." Well, why not? White people haven't made such a grand job of governing themselves. Why are they bothering about the Samoans?'

'How did you get on at Falefa?' asked a man who had just squeezed himself into a few inches of space between me and the pig. 'Did you get the *inganga*? I saw you going out there in the car in the rain. I bet you got wet!'

'Soaked,' I said, 'drowned! But plenty of *inganga*.'

'How the hell do those little fish get up that fifty feet of waterfall?' he asked. 'I've been there when they were running, and I've seen 'em skipping up the face of that cliff. How can a fish cling to the side of a rock?'

'They've got suckers,' I said. 'Two of the fins on their belly have turned into a sucker.'

'Never saw anything like it—millions of 'em, no bigger than that,' he said, holding up a match. 'Skip, skip, wriggle, skip!'

The *inganga*, to which he referred, are the fry of a fresh-water fish, the *apofu*, that spends the early stages of its career in the sea. With the first floods of the rainy season, they ascend the streams in millions. At this time their pelvic fins are modified into a sucking disk which enables them to cling to vertical or even overhanging surfaces. Of those that I kept alive, many clung to the sides of the jar, above water level. All were exceedingly active and could leap a foot or more into the air even from dry ground. Like the *palolo*, they are considered a great delicacy, and, during the few days of the year when they are running up from the sea, the natives go to the waterfalls and brush them into sacks.

The beginning of the wet season is indeed a happy time for the epicure. Not only do the *palolo* and the *inganga* appear, with deep-water fish entering the lagoon in search of them, but there is a small and succulent land crab, the *mali'o*, which on one night of the year migrates from its pools among the tree roots far inland, for spawning. In armies they march towards the sea, a moving carpet on the ground. Nothing deflects them from their course. Through villages and even through houses they will go in their blind intent. The natives know when to expect them and, by the light of torches, make slaughter for a mighty feast.

'There's the store, ahead of us,' said Harry, as we rounded a point of the coast some fifteen miles from the town. 'It's not mine any longer. Sold it a few years back to Mata Miller, and bought a spot of land. Got enough money coming from England these times, some in this letter now, to buy tobacco. That's all a man wants, if he has a bit of land and a family to work it.'

The bus creaked to a halt beside the store, and we clambered out. '*Talofa*, Mata!' called Harry to a man who was sitting half asleep on the veranda. 'This way,' he said to me, taking the lead on a narrow track beside the house. We hadn't gone a hundred yards among the palms when a coco-nut hit the ground between us with a thud. Two seconds earlier or later and one of us would have been finished. Harry took off his hat and looked at it carefully. 'Don't want that hurt,' he said, stroking it affectionately. 'My brother brought that hat from Niue. He died on the ship that took him back. Yes, he died on board, and, a funny thing, my wife knew—yes, she knew all right. One day, soon after he sailed, I came in from the plantation and she said to me: "Johnny is dead." I said: "What you talk about? Johnny is half-way to Niue." She said: "One hour ago he walk in here, and he look all around. He see your hat on the table and he take it up and he smile. Then he put it down again and he go out. I go after him and I call, but he not there. I think he dead." Two months after that we get letter—Johnny dead on ship.'

We went on over rough and rising ground. In a patch

41

of swamp were some taro plants, in some stony ground were coffee bushes. 'That's a pretty good rubber plantation over there,' said Harry, pointing across a valley. 'Worth your while to go there, see the whole job in ten minutes. Boys come in with the stuff from the trees, like milk—thick milk, and they pour it out into a big old bath they pinched from somewhere, and they add a drop of water, and then they bucket it out into wooden trays. And next day that stuff is a rubber mat; and they shove it through a few mangles to flatten it a bit, and then they hang it up in a shed full of wood smoke, and after a few days they pack it in bales and off it goes. Folks say it's best rubber in the Islands.'

As we entered a plantation of cocoa-trees, with their heavy pods of yellow, crimson, and purple growing grotesquely on their branches, the track widened into a grass path, at the end of which I could see a wooden building. 'Here we are,' said Harry. The nearer we got to the house the more ramshackle it appeared. On close acquaintance it seemed that at any moment it might resolve itself into a pile of firewood. In front of it there were a few untended flower-beds on what might once have been a lawn. Some twenty yards away a girl sat under a trickling tap, washing herself, unconcerned at our approach. In Samoa they bath, as we bathe, at any hour of the day.

Harry's Samoan wife beamed a welcome from the nearby cookhouse as she adjusted her *lavalava* above richly cambered curves. Daughters, too, appeared, beaming and buxom as their mother, and sons, and sons-in-law, darkskinned and vigorous, and many small children of the next generation.

The house was of two rooms only, one above the other. In the lower one, which was completely open on the garden side, there were two rusty iron bedsteads and a table. Upstairs, whither I was taken almost immediately, by an outside ladder, the furnishings were more elaborate. In addition to a roll of sleeping mats in one corner and a mattress on the floor, there was a large home-made arm-chair, as well as a sea-chest with a broken lid, and several wooden boxes. 'You sit in the chair,' said Harry, 'I like the floor.' Scattered about the room were clubs, paddles, spears, and picture frames, mostly broken. 'From Fiji,'

said Harry, as he saw me looking at a club on the wall, 'made from a young tree, one of the kind with the roots sticking out like plates. The head is the roots and the handle is the stem. Look at the nicks on the handle, down near the head, twenty-one of them. There's some nice stories there for you if you knew all about them. That fish-hook, alongside, is a famous one. It had a name once, but I 've forgotten it. What do you think of that for a fine mat? Twenty strands to the inch. Take years to make. My wife brought it along when we got married.'

I had known before of the value attached to fish-hooks, especially those of pearl shell. A good bonito hook is only perfected after many weeks of skilled craftsmanship, and some, through a slight difference of colour or shape, may be much more successful than others. It is these successful ones which soon become talked of and widely known, and are given a special name. Samoans refer to a man who has become a celebrity as 'like a famous hook.'

According to ancient custom a visiting chief may ask to see the fish-hooks of his host. Should he then admire any one of those spread before him, the owner is in honour bound to give it to him. A hook that is lost in this way may be a source of scheming and intrigue for many years. Visit after visit will be paid to successive owners by successive accomplices until eventually, wits having outwitted wits, the hook is again in its original owner's possession. But any hooks attached to a rod are safe from such depredation, and for this reason a chief rich in hooks may often fasten to his rod an even greater number of hooks than are necessary to meet the varying tints of sea and sky.

When I suggested to Harry that I should make a drawing of the club, then and there, he said: 'No, you take it with you. Take the fish-hook, too. I 'll come along fetch 'em one day.' As he spoke he opened the sea-chest and began to pull out quantities of dusty insect-eaten papers and other oddments. 'Here you are, you can have that,' he said, handing me a tattooing comb that had fallen from among the papers. 'The teeth are from a bit of a pig's tusk. In the old days they liked a bit of a man's hip bone.' Loose sheets of paper and rolls of legal documents tumbled on to the floor. There were pages of unpublished manuscripts written by his father; there were letters dealing with long-forgotten local politics; there were photographs of East Anglian social gatherings of the late nineteenth century, and there were crested invitations to official functions of that period in England. 'Look at this,' said Harry, handing me a photograph of a military parade. '"Blessing the colours"; and the missionaries came here and shouted because the heathens blessed the war clubs.'

Harry couldn't find what he was looking for, yet everything that he pulled out of that chest called for comment. More and more of his family came and sat about the room as he talked. Naked children sprawled among the papers. But time was running on, and I was thinking about getting home.

'Don't you worry,' said Harry, 'we 'll hold the bus for you.'

He pulled out miniatures of ancestors, indifferently painted but attributed to great masters. Romney and

44

Gainsborough were discredited with travesties imputed to their hands. There was a torn photograph of Robert Louis Stevenson, heavily bearded, taken at Vailima, with Mrs. Stevenson sitting cross-legged on the floor in voluminous skirts. 'You've been to Vailima. Have you heard the ghost?' asked Harry.

'I've heard tapping over the mantelpiece, near where he used to sit,' I said, 'but some think it's rats.'

'Rats be damned,' he said, 'it's Stevenson. You go and stay there. Sometimes of an evening you'll see him walk up the stairs into that room. What about this?' he asked, throwing me a sheet of paper. 'That's a third verse of the poem on his grave, but they didn't use it.'

'Here shall the winds about me blow.
Here the clouds shall come and go.
Here shall be peace for evermo',
And the heart for aye shall be still.'

Cockroaches scrambled from the box as Harry disturbed its lower layers. Lizards' eggs, like large pearls, dropped from the papers as he handled them. At last, the last of everything in the chest, 'the family plant.' This was what he had brought me from Apia to see. Fourteen generations direct from Henry VII, including six earls, one duke, a bishop, and four rectors. 'That's the bishop,' said Harry, pointing to an engraving that, in its broken frame, leant against the wall.

'You see,' he said, handing me the 'plant.' 'Henry VII had a son called Henry VIII. That's not important. The line you've got to follow is his daughter, Mary. She married Louis XII of France. He's not important, either. But when he died she married Charles Brandon, Duke of Suffolk, and that *is* important—that's where I come in. I'm not special particular about these things, and I always say a man's not responsible for the bed he was born in; but, all in all, and after all, as you might say, there's only a few of us come from the best beds.'

Then he showed me the gold signet ring of the family,

and the copies of its armorial bearings which he had compelled each of his seven half-native sons to complete. We were deep in a heraldic discussion, concerning not only Honourable Ordinaries, Tinctures, Blazonings, Marshallings, Cadency, and Differencing, but also the identity of the curious quadruped that had been copied so laboriously on to the seven shields, with strangely varying results, when I felt a nudge at my elbow. One of his daughters was offering me food—on a plate, tin, enamelled, a demi-duck, rampant, congealed in onions. But almost at the same moment I heard voices of heralds, without, proclaiming that a bus had been sighted from the hill-top. Immediately a messenger was dispatched to stay it in its course.

Harry wrapped the contents of the plate in a banana leaf and thrust it, with the club, the fish-hook, and the tattooing comb, among the drawing materials in my haversack. At the foot of the ladder a son was ready to carry the haversack; two daughters were there to decorate me with *ulas* of frangipane. When I reached the bus another son was waiting for me with a basket of fresh-water crayfish, and as I stepped inside the vehicle the driver pointed to a hank of bananas which he said was mine.

Sic itur ad Apia, as my maternal grandfather's scutcheon nearly said.

CHAPTER SEVEN

ONCE UPON A TIME a crab, a bird, and a rat decided to go for a sail in a coco-nut shell. It was a lovely day, as calm as you please when they set out, and the wind was carrying them along gently and sweetly on the smooth waters of the lagoon. But all of a sudden a storm blew up. It was a very big storm, so big, indeed, that in no time at all the coco-nut shell filled to the top and sank. The crab didn't mind this very much because, apart from the picnic being spoiled, he suffered no inconvenience. He just dropped to the bottom with the coco-nut shell, and made himself at home below. The bird—a plover, such as any one may see in Europe—didn't mind either, because, just before its feet got wet, it opened its wings and flew away. For the rat matters were more serious. It was a long swim to shore and the sea had really got very rough. Things looked bad and the rat became very frightened. But just when he was beginning to give up all hope an octopus came along.

'Come and sit on my head,' said the octopus.

'Thanks very much, that will do me nicely,' said the rat.

So the rat climbed on to the head of the octopus and sat down and made himself as comfortable as he could, while the octopus swam towards the shore. This was pure good nature on the part of the octopus; his actions had nothing whatever behind them but sheer kindness of heart. Unfortunately, the rat had few manners, and on his way to the shore he not only forgot the few he had but he behaved in a really rude and shocking way. To make matters worse, no sooner had he got safely ashore than he called to the octopus: 'See what I have left on your head.' With his eight arms the octopus had, of course, no difficulty in finding out what had happened, and as might be expected —and most justifiably, I consider—he flew into a rage. An octopus in a rage is a frightening spectacle. I 've seen one myself, writhing with anger, every colour of the rainbow shooting up and down its long tentacles in quick succession, and its hundreds of suckers gripping at everything, and its parrot-like jaws gnashing, and its wild madcow-like eyes darting glances of hate. But that is by the way. This octopus of which I write soon realized that self-control is a much more effective weapon than blind rage, and that was long before the missionaries came to Samoa, which speaks well for the octopus. He therefore called to the owls of the island: 'Come, owls of the sea, come, owls of the land, come, owls of the east, come, owls of the west. Come seek the rat, the rat that I hate, the rat that has no manners.' Thereupon from north, south, east, and west the owls came, and one of them, quite a youngster, put his foot into the burrow of a sand crab and hauled out the very rat that had been so ungrateful. A moment later there weren't as much as two hairs of its fur sticking together.

Now scientists may say that you cannot inherit acquired characteristics, but scientists don't know everything—not yet. The patent, palpable, living fact is that, ever since that unhappy picnic party, every octopus on the reef is filled with hate the moment he sees a rat. He rushes at it and seizes it and holds on to it, regardless of any danger to his own life, in an effort to wipe out the insult to his family. Here I could digress on blood feuds in Spain, in Scotland, in Sardinia, in Samoa, but like the octopus I will exercise self-control. The point of this story is that on any calm day in Samoa, morning or evening, you may see a fisherman in his canoe, paddling with his left hand while with his right he dangles in the water the facsimile of a rat, made of shells and fibre; and if you watch but a short while you will see an octopus lifted into the canoe, clinging tightly to its mortal enemy. Many times I have seen this from the shore, many times I have been in the canoe with the fisherman, and many times afterwards, even on islands a thousand miles away, I have heard the same story. It must be true.

CHAPTER EIGHT

CHARLIE HAD MADE all arrangements for my visit to Sa'anapu, even to finding a new orator, Lavasi'i, to replace my earlier official who had since gone to Tutuila. Though Lavasi'i was tall and of great dignity, there were times when he reminded me of a spaniel, as he sat, almost 'to heel,' awaiting my slightest gesture of command. As long as I stayed in Upolu he was at my service, and nothing pleased him more than the suggestion of a new journey. My prestige was his prestige, and he never underrated either of us in his negotiations.

But Charlie's messages had gone astray, and twice the guest house at Sa'anapu had been decorated in vain. However, Lauvi, my host, did not think anything of that— 'the girls had nothing else to do,' he said. Now that I had arrived he hoped I would spend many weeks in his village. He gave a warm welcome to us all.

Lauvi is close on seventy years of age, but still full of vigour. On the morning of my arrival he had been climbing coco-nut palms to pick nuts for sennit-making. 'You must get the ones with the long fibres in the husk,' he told me. The day before he had gone out in his canoe, alone, and speared a shark. Though not very tall, he has a tremendous depth of chest. From a deeply wrinkled face his eyes radiate benignity. Around his domed head, richly tanned by the sun, there is a halo of crisp white curls. For twenty years he has been *pulenu'u*—magistrate of the village; though elections are held every three years, there has never been any question of a change since he was first chosen.

He had met us on the road about two miles from the village, and as he led the way along the rough track through the bush he took delight in pointing out the various patches of his plantations: taro, bananas, cocoa, coffee. He still made copra, splitting open the ripe coco-nuts and digging out the flesh: he reckoned he could make and carry back three loads of it in the day. Each load would weigh about a hundred and fifty pounds.

Half a mile from our destination we clambered over the stone wall that keeps some of the pigs out of the village, and soon afterwards reached an inner lagoon across which a perilous causeway of palm trunks wound its way to the opposite shore. The tide was low and, here, people were washing their clothes and themselves and drawing water from springs that would be covered at high tide. From the end of the causeway a short walk through bush led us to the village, spread along the shore, with palms and flowering trees interspersed among the houses on the sandy ground.

We were greeted in the customary way with a kava ceremony, after which Lauvi and the other chiefs retired, leaving us to rest while a meal was prepared. Later in the evening he came back. He wanted to know if he might hold the family prayers in my house. Even as he spoke young men, women, and children crowded into the *fale*, sitting respectfully on the ground at the far end. They sang a hymn, Lauvi's orator read a passage from the Bible, and then Lauvi began to pray.

'Let us give thanks to God this evening. Our hearts are overflowing with happiness because many days we look for the Tusitala and now he is come. May God strengthen his body and preserve his health. It is hard for travellers in a strange land, very far from home. May he come to a true knowledge of this village and its people during his stay with us. We offer thanks that the cricket games at Saluafata have ended without any unhappy fighting, and we pray that our young men may come back in safety. We know that the accident on the road to-day was due to the stupidness of the girl who was in the way of the truck, but we ask that you will give a blessing to the doctors in Apia who are looking after her broken leg. May the cool winds that are now blowing give us all the good health.'

That ended the prayers. The women left the *fale*, but the children remained with us. For a while Lauvi sat and talked. He wanted to know if it was true that there were no coco-nut palms in England. If so, what did we drink in the dry season? How many days had it taken me to come from England? He had never been further than Apia. In the old times that used to be a long and tiring journey, by boat and through the bush, but it was better now that they had the new cross-island road. Had we roads as good as that in England, wide enough for two trucks to pass? He told me that the greatest happiness in his life had been at the birth of his first male child, the greatest sadness at the death of a younger son. Fishing had always been his delight, but he also enjoyed working on his plantation. To-morrow they would be going fishing on the reef. Perhaps I would like to go with them.

Then he excused himself, saying that I must be tired and would like to get to bed. 'Let the old man's boat move inland,' he said, getting up. It is an expression used at sea if there is any danger of a storm—the old men had better go first. Mats were unrolled on the floor for Charlie and Lavasi'i; curtains of tapa cloth had been let down to screen my bed.

But next day there was a deluge of rain. There could be no fishing. From dawn onwards the squalls had increased, at times blowing the rain almost horizontally across the *malae*—the open space in the centre of the village. Limpetlike, the houses clung to their stony platforms. Except for small openings on the sheltered side, all the blinds were let down and made fast. Men climbed on to the roofs and fastened coco-nut fronds over weak places in the thatch, or hung banana stalks or baulks of wood across the ridge. Palms with their yielding fronds were like umbrellas blown inside out; wind-whipped bushes like cattle with their backs to the storm. When for a moment sunlight broke through the clouds, children emerged from the *fales* like hermit crabs from their shells, scurrying here and there, naked, splashing in the pools. Women went by, laughing and jesting, their clothes drenched and torn. The booming of the surf on the reef was like the distant rumble of wagons in convoy.

By midday the wind had dropped, but the rain continued to fall, straight as a plumb-line, a heavy thunderous downpour. For me it was the chance of a fresh-water bath. By the time I reached the shore I was wet enough to wash. After a good lather, a swim in the lagoon removed the soap, and then two minutes in the rain removed the salt water. When I re-entered the *fale*, Tupe, one of my attendant maidens, was there, preparing the table for lunch. It didn't matter to her that I wanted to dry myself and dress; those are things that any Samoan can do in public with perfect propriety. Anyway, her thoughts were far away. For long periods she would stand gazing abstractedly out of the *fale*. Then she would rearrange the knife,  fork, and plate on the table, then she would rearrange her hair; then she would move the flowers on the table, taking one of them and putting it in her hair, then she would relax again and rest after her efforts. Her first job every morning, even before she brought my breakfast, was to sit on the floor of the house with baskets of hibiscus and frangipane blooms, and thread them on to the midribs of coco-nut frondlets which she stuck into coco-nut husks filled with sand. Silau, her friend, often helped her in her domestic duties. Together, it would take them half an hour to wash up the few things I had used at table. Silau would sit cross-legged before an enamel basin while Tupe, beside her, would ladle water into it from a bucket. Then, very slowly, each plate or knife or cup would be taken and washed. Tupe would do the drying even more slowly, polishing the same plate over and over again.

After lunch the weather suddenly cleared. Clouds still hung above the mountains, and wraiths of mist encircled the peaks, but overhead the sky was blue. A message came to me that I was to receive a food presentation —a mark of special respect, as to a visiting chief. No sooner had the messenger departed than Lauvi appeared, heading a procession. He was wearing ceremonial tapa cloth over his cotton *lavalava*, and carried in his hand a coco-nut. Beside him walked his orator. Entering my *fale* he put the coco-nut on the ground before me; then removing his tapa cloth he laid that beside the nut. Then came a young man bearing cooked taro and a chicken, on a woven tray; and after him another bearer with a pig, cooked whole, in a basket. All these offerings were presented to me as I sat in state between Lavasi'i and Charlie. Then Lauvi's orator made a speech, explaining the symbolism of the food, drink and clothing that had been given to me. At the same time, Lavasi'i, exercising his prerogative as orator, appropriated the coco-nut and the tapa cloth. One eye of the nut had been pierced and, through this, Lavasi'i drank noisily—the more noise on these occasions, the more correct. Having drunk, he broke the nut on the stones of the house platform, again as noisily as possible, thereby announcing to the village that this presentation had been made. In olden times coco-nuts were only broken in this manner for the gods: to-day they are broken thus only for the highest chiefs. Lavasi'i then went outside and from the platform of the house called to the whole village, announcing who had made the presentation, and who had been honoured. He then made a speech on my behalf, thanking Lauvi and his family for their generosity, after which Lauvi's orator replied, belittling the gifts. It is a point of honour in Samoan etiquette always to belittle what they give, always to exaggerate what they receive. Again and again in my wanderings, after I had been shown the most profuse hospitality, I was told how they would like to have done much more, but that owing to the weather, or because they had had short notice of my visit, or for a variety of other reasons, they had been unable to do half what they would have liked to do. On the other hand, public announcements of any small presents that I had made in the way of 'Fiji biscuits,' *pisupo*, or *lavalavas*, were always doubled if not, at times, trebled. Why tinned beef should be called *pisupo* in Samoa I have never been able to discover. Even the purveyors of it do not know. Further east among the islands the same product is known as *bulamakau*, that name being derived from a 'bull-an'-a-cow' left in Tonga by Captain Cook.

When my visitors had retired it was Lavasi'i's duty to carve the pig and see to its proper distribution. There had to be one portion for the *faifeau*, the pastor; another for the doctor; others went to the chiefs of the village and to the orators, according to rank; not forgetting the cooks, and the village *taupou*. There was not a little local feeling about the portion for the *faifeau*. Every day, from every oven in the village, he gets his share, perhaps twenty baskets in all, and always the best. 'The portion for God,' he calls it. In at the front door it goes and, most of it, out at the back, to his pigs.

'All the time same thing,' said Charlie. 'One day the *faifeau* in Le'ile'i village tell folk in church: "God want canoe." He say: "You go make canoe for God, big bonito canoe." So all the men in the village help make bonito canoe. Then *faifeau* say: "Thanks very much, I use it for God."'

In any village in Samoa, if you want to find the pastor's house seek the biggest. The vocation brings prosperity; so much so that it is often said among the people: 'It cannot last. He cannot have it both times.' One of them remarked to me: 'When he die, that finish—he have all his good time in Samoa.' Because of this worldly success, it is not unusual to-day for a father to bury the umbilical cord of his new-born son under or near a church in the hope that the boy will become a pastor, just as sometimes he will bury it in a plantation if he wishes him to be a successful cultivator of the soil, or sink it in the sea in a shell if he wishes him to achieve success as a fisherman. In the Cook Islands a father will often preserve the *pito*, as it is called, in the hope that one day he may be able to drop it into the sacred waters of Raiatea harbour, and thus invoke safety at sea for his child. Alternatively, he may carry it far out to sea and drop it into deep water, thereby hoping to ensure longevity. In Tonga the cord of a girl is usually buried in a mound near to the house, sweet-scented flowers being planted over it so that she may be fragrant as the blossoms; that of a boy is buried at the root of an ancient tree that can defy a storm.

When the ceremony was over I was free to wander along the beach. The untrodden sand was cool after the rain. On one side the lagoon, iridescent as a *tiotala's* wing, on the other side dense bush, soaked and silent. The leaves of the palms hung limp, scarcely a frond stirred. A blue heron was stepping delicately in the shallow water, a black pig was routing in the debris above the tide mark. A paddle lost when fishing, a broken fish trap, a coil of sennit rope, lay where the tide had left them.

A mile from the village I found a pool of liquid turquoise set in the black enamel of time-polished lava. Over its margin spread great branches of the broad-leafed *futu* trees, dripping their crimson-tipped ivory tassels into the water.

I thought as I approached that I heard splashing in the pool. I thought, later, that I heard a boy's voice and a girl's laughter in the bush. That was the only hint I ever had of love-making in Samoa—not, of course, that they are idle.

As I returned dusk was falling. Palm-trees and *fales* were fading into a smoky monotone with the sand. All light and colour seemed drained from the village and poured into the sea. Children were hurrying home through tracks in the bush. They do not like to be far from the village at night. They say that ghosts wander, many of them in the form of dogs or cats or birds.

Later that evening Lauvi came to my *fale*, again, for prayers. He gave especial thanks that the young men of the village had all reached home in safety after the cricket games. He gave thanks that we had been sheltered and preserved in the face of the great rain. He said he knew well that many of the roofs had long needed attention. He gave thanks for our continued health and strength. 'It is well understood,' he said, 'that health of mind is most important, especially for Europeans who have this special skill of travelling from one country to another.'

CHAPTER NINE

IT WAS RAINING again next morning, heavily but without wind. Through the steady drip and splatter from the thatch on to the stones below I could hear the rhythmic hammering of tapa mallets. It was not unlike the drumming of gold-beaters at work. I thought of an office I had once visited in London, a gold-beaters' office. There, lying on the desk, was a long coiled ribbon of yellow metal, rather more than an inch in width and scarcely as thick as a visiting card. 'Gold, just gold,' said Mr. Whiley, whose family had been gold-beaters for more than a century. Then he took me into the workshop. There must have been a hundred men there, each hammering away at his little pile of gold-beater's skins which, five inches square and interleaved with gold, he held on the marble anvil before him. 'One inch square it starts from, cut from the ribbon,' said Mr. Whiley. 'Each one is beaten to four times its size; then it is cut into four and each of the pieces is beaten again; then they are cut a second time and beaten, and again a third time. You get sixty-four sheets, four inches by four, from one square inch of ribbon. At the first beatings they are interleaved with vellum, later with "gold-beater's skin"—from the intestine of an ox.' A thousand of these skins are beaten at a time, each interleaved with gold, a mould he called it. He took a leaf and held it to the light; London was visible through it, as through dark green glass. 'Two hundred and fifty thousand to the inch,' he said. Yet those gossamer sheets have density enough to shine with splendour from the dome of St. Paul's or to embellish the palaces of kings, as in former times similar sheets, if only slightly thicker, overlaid the Ark of the Covenant and adorned the tombs of the Pharaohs.

The noise of the mallets came from a *fale* close to mine. In it an elderly woman was sitting cross-legged before a sloping board, on which she was scraping long strips of the inner bark of the paper mulberry shrub. This is the same plant whose bark is used to-day in Japan to make that paper, so exquisite for proofing engravings, and which, according to Marco Polo, was used in the thirteenth century by the Kublai Khan at his mint in the city of Cambaluc, the modern Pekin, to make his much-inflated currency.

At the other end of the *fale* a girl was sitting before a baulk of wood on which she was beating the scraped bark into thin sheets. Not far from her two other women were building these sheets into a tough and pliable material. Using a tuber of arrowroot for paste, they added one layer of the tissue to another, dusting all the while with red ochreous earth, and rubbing lightly, as one takes impressions from ancient brasses. When finished, the incised pattern of the board on which they worked was printed in the fabric.

In the next *fale* a dozen women were weaving mats. Some were making rough floor mats from coco-nut fronds; others were making sleeping mats of a narrower weft, from pandanus leaves—full length for adults and smaller for babies. A mother or a grandmother shows her affection for a child by the care she puts into the making of these small mats. Most important of all, a few of the older women were making Fine Mats. These may take years to complete, and are treasured possessions, even heirlooms. Their weave is fine as Kerry homespun, their texture soft as Belfast linen. They constitute the wealth of a family, the dowry of brides. Agreements are ratified by their exchange. Their value increases with age, for in their changes of ownership lies the history of villages. Names are given to the most famous, and songs composed in their honour.

I left Charlie among the women while I returned to my *fale* to make a drawing of a stone that, once used for sharpening stone adzes, was now a mortar for kava-pounding. As I finished the drawing, he came in, smiling. He said the women wanted to know if I had been to Fiji. If so, had I any of the oil with me? A little of that and they'd soon fix all the boys and girls of the village. If he

c

could get some of it from me, he could have any girl he
liked on the island. Yes, they knew all about the leaves
and the hairs from the girl's head, and a drop of the man's
blood. But it was the oil, the special oil from Fiji that

was wanted. It was no good without the oil. He said that
they 'd been talking about a girl who was *taupou* of a
village on Savai'i. No one had ever spoken a word against
her character; every one knew she was a true *taupou*. But
one day a boy who had been in Fiji came along and he
took a fancy to her, and he mixed up some leaves with
some of the oil that he had, and when she wasn't looking
he put a few drops of it on her hair. That night she crept
in to him in his *fale*. But he was so scared, because she was
a *taupou*, that he ran away, and he never came back to that
village. Nobody in her village knew what had happened.
The women had only heard about it from a friend of the
boy's. They thought that in his fright he had thrown
away the bottle. They wished they knew where he had
thrown it.

Later in the morning Lauvi came to see me. He did not
seem to be in his usual good spirits. When I inquired if
anything was wrong, he told me he was worried because
he had just heard that a former chief of the village had been
carrying a local dispute to Apia. That was against all
tradition. For a long time this man had not been behaving
as one in his position should behave. He was not respecting
the old customs. Though a titular chief he would sometimes take the place of an orator. That was not right.
Neither was it right when he caught a turtle that he should
refuse to divide it, ceremonially, with the other chiefs.

The turtle is a sacred fish, and must be treated as such. His action was a deliberate insult to the village. He had also made trouble about the wearing of a *tuinga*, the head-dress permitted only to those of special rank and status. Finally, and more serious still, he had attempted to seize land. A few weeks earlier Lauvi and his fellow chiefs had held a council, at which, after reviewing all these incidents, they had pronounced judgment. Four orators were deputed to convey the verdict to the offender. These four men, each with his ceremonial staff, had then gone to his house and, standing outside, had announced to him that, for all time unto eternity, his title and all his honours had been taken from him. He was no longer a chief. His kava title, too, and all other privileges of a chief, were no longer his. Whether he stayed in the village or went elsewhere was for him to choose; but if he stayed in the village he did so as an untitled man.

The man left the village. But now, contrary to all tradition, he had carried his grievance to the governor. That was what was worrying Lauvi—the disregard of tradition. Lauvi left me to attend a council on the subject.

The rain continued throughout the afternoon. Without any wind it was possible to have the sides of the house open. But there was little to see. Water dripping from the thatch made a curtain of lace around the house.

Lavasi'i slept and snored. Charlie sat on the floor, rolling and smoking endless cigarettes. I was trying to read a copy of the Rev. J. B. Stair's *Old Samoa*. Stair had come to Samoa as a missionary in 1838, and his book gives us one of the best records of the island culture at that time.

Charlie kept interrupting me. From a scrap of paper in which his tobacco had been wrapped, he read some of the fines recently imposed at the court in Apia. 'Taking delivery of cocoa beans, not of good quality: £5. Taking delivery of undried fermenting copra: £5. Committing adultery: £1. Sitting on the road: 5s.' He said he had once been fined £3 in Tonga for playing clock golf on a

Sunday. He was nearly fined £5 there for being without a shirt on the public road, but they let him off as he was new to the island. He said there was a law on the statute book in Tonga that if a man became thirsty when travelling he might pick a coco-nut for drinking from any tree beside the road, no matter to whom the tree belonged. The same was true in Samoa, only there was no written law about it. A few minutes later, he told me that the best cure for wasp or bee stings was a green banana. 'Cut it in two and rub the cut end on the sting,' he said.

But, apart from these irrelevancies, it was Stair's account of his personal experiences with the occult that was occupying my thoughts. In telling of them he writes: 'I was at length forced to the conclusion that they were the result of other than ordinary agencies.' He tells of a 'succession of extraordinary noises and visitations' that occurred at Falelatai, a village twelve miles along the coast to the west of Sa'anapu, which he 'could never understand or fathom as arising from any ordinary cause.' Night after night, when he and his family had gone to bed, the passage which ran from end to end of his house, a new building, 'appeared to be taken possession of by a party of bowlers who kept up an incessant rolling from end to end. . . . At other times loud knockings and noises would be heard at the outer doors . . . but not the slightest trace could be found of the delinquents.' He goes on to tell of events which made a particularly strong impression on his mind.

'It was a lovely moonlight night, and a number of natives, chiefs and leading men, had gathered in my front room, as their delight was, to talk over various matters, especially to discuss foreign customs and doings. The room was full, and we were in the midst of an animated discussion, when suddenly a tremendous crash came at the front door, as though it must be smashed in. Instantly the whole party jumped up and scattered, some to the front, some to the back, and others to the ends of the house, so as to surround it effectually and capture the aggressor; and as some of the natives were sitting close to the door they were outside in a few seconds. Not a soul was to be seen out-side, however; and in a very short time the whole party were collected together again, very crestfallen and dis-appointed at their want of success, as well as keenly dis-cussing who could have caused the noise. The idea of its being the act of a native was scouted by the whole party, who said it was well known that the gathering of leading men was there, and that no native would have dared to commit the outrage.

'It was at length generally conceded that it must be the doings of the *aitu* or *aitus*, who were such constant aggressors. Yet, for all that, every place, likely and un-likely, was still further keenly searched, but without avail. Later on in the evening we were all collected together at one end of the building near to a large *ifi* (chestnut-tree), in which a good-sized bell was hung for various purposes. Suddenly this bell began to ring violently, without any apparent cause. No hand was pulling it, but it kept on wildly clanging, in full view of the whole party who looked on in amazement. "Perhaps there is a string attached, and someone pulling it who is hidden under that stone wall," suggested one of the party. One of the number imme-diately ran to the fence; no one there! Another climbed the tree. There was no string attached, but the bell kept wildly ringing. There was in reality no need to climb the tree to ascertain the fact of there being no string attached to the bell, for every leaf and twig stood out to view most distinctly in the bright moonlight. The mystery was not solved, and the old conclusion was again come to, that it was part of the mischievous doings of the *aitu*. . . . Some thought the house had been unwittingly placed upon an old native burying-ground. Others suggested that the *ifi* tree was an old *malumalu*, or temple of an *aitu*. If so, the wrath of the various *folaunga aitu*, or parties of voyaging spirits, must have been stirred at seeing the sanctity of their temple thus invaded.'

Whatever the cause of these troubles, the author felt compelled to leave the house, and only after he had moved to another part of the island did he and his family find peace of mind.

He ends his chapter by saying: 'I find it impossible to rest satisfied with the conclusion that it was "flesh and blood,"' and he quotes the words of St. Paul: 'Our wrestling is not against flesh and blood, but against the principalities, against the powers, against the world-rulers of this darkness, against the spiritual hosts of wickedness in the heavenly places.'

I asked Charlie if he had ever seen anything of this kind, and he said he had heard people talking about such things in many different places, but he had never paid much attention to them. When Lauvi came to my *fale* later, I asked him the same question, and he had much to say. Had I never heard of *vai aitu*, ghost medicine? he inquired.

Sometimes, he said, the spirit of a dead man or woman will enter the body of a relative who has evaded some duty to the family, and that person will become ill, and will die unless the spirit, the *aitu*, can be persuaded to leave. It is very difficult to do this, only someone very skilled can manage it—each wise man has his own method. Usually certain leaves are beaten up or chewed, and then with water added are strained through the sheath of a coco-nut frond. The liquid is rubbed all over the sufferer, and some of it is dropped into the openings of the body, and then the wise man addresses the *aitu*, asking for its name and the reasons why the sick person has been troubled. Usually the *aitu* will answer, speaking through the mouth of the sick person, but with its own voice. Then, when the relatives have learned of the offence, they promise suitable compensation, and after that the *aitu* will depart. But sometimes it will refuse to answer and will stay in the body, the sick person all the time getting worse. When eventually it does leave the body the patient dies immediately. There had been one particularly difficult case within the past few years. Death after death had occurred in the same family, and eventually two further members of it, an orator and his brother, fell ill. Several wise men were consulted, and each in turn did his best but without success. After much discussion it was decided that some measure more powerful than the ordinary *vai aitu* must be employed. A party of friends, therefore, went to the village cemetery and at mid-day, in the presence of many villagers, disinterred the bones of the woman whose *aitu* was thought to be causing the trouble. These bones, together with certain bitter leaves, were boiled over an open fire for three hours, and were then taken beyond the reef and thrown into the deep water. After that the orator and his brother made a quick recovery, and the family have not since been troubled.

I was told, too, of the mother of one of the girls who were looking after my house. One Friday morning, about eight o'clock, she had left the village with another woman to go into the bush to collect wild banana leaves for the oven. The bush was dense, so much so that in fear of getting lost the two women kept calling to each other as they chopped the leaves. Suddenly the mother realized that it was not her friend but a stranger who was answering her. In fear she hurried towards the village. But she had only gone a short distance when she found herself stopped, as if by some presence, some invisible being. In what-ever direction she tried to go she was turned back. All through the day she struggled, powerless, to break through this imprisoning force. Then, when she saw that dark-ness was coming, she built herself a shelter of fallen fronds and slept under it during the night. Next morning there was still no release, and again, all through the day she kept walking backwards and forwards without avail. She slept in the same shelter during the second night. But on the third day, the Sunday, she felt a sudden freedom. There was no longer any obstructing power. She was able to return to the village. During all that time in the bush she had seen no one, but during each night she had heard the voices of her dead father and brother saying to her: 'You must care for your brother who lives.' That was all they said. Three times each night each of them had repeated those words: 'You must care for your brother who lives.'

Meanwhile all the village had been searching for the woman, calling and blowing conch shells to attract her attention, but she had heard none of them. They had sent for a wise man and he had gone into the bush and gathered leaves. These he had put into a glass of water and had held it up to the light, and because the leaves changed colour he said that the woman would return. But, also, in church the pastor had prayed, and it was soon after that that the woman returned. Many of the people thought that she had come back because of the prayers, but there were many also who thought it might be because of the *vai aitu*.

Late that evening it was still raining. In his prayer Lauvi asked that there might soon be a change of weather. 'As of course you know,' he said, 'it is not the wet season, and there have now been many days of great rain. It is difficult for the Tusitala to learn the ways of our village.'

As I looked beyond him towards the sea, I could distinguish a faint light on the horizon as if the clouds were lifting.

CHAPTER TEN

NEXT MORNING the sky was clear, the sun was shining. I had hardly finished breakfast when I received another food presentation, fifteen baskets in all, this time from the chiefs of the village. The earlier presentation had been a family affair from my host. Six orators brought the gifts, and there was much ceremony and speech-making, not only in the presentation of the food to me, but in my distribution of it, through Lavasi'i, immediately afterwards.

One chief in the village had omitted to send a contribution. But there was no slight in this: he was having a house built, and that precluded him from making any gifts of food, tapa cloth, or fine mats to any one but the builders. It is one of the many recognized terms in the agreement between the prospective owner of a house and the carpenters whom he employs.

Like every undertaking of any importance in Samoa, the building of a house cannot be accomplished without a great deal of ceremony. Only members of the highly honoured guild may be employed, and they must be treated throughout the operation not only with the greatest respect but with many observances which to the unconversant might seem irrational. A big feast is held at the commencement of the work, another on its completion, and many lesser celebrations as various stages in the construction are reached. There is tremendous pride of craftsmanship among the carpenters, and rightly so—the Samoans are the architects of the Pacific. Nowhere else among the Islands will one see the same dignity of design or an equal perfection of finish in the work.

After lunch that day a message came to me that there was to be a fishing expedition. Men with diving goggles on their heads and spears in their hands were already passing along the beach towards their canoes; women with baskets and poles were wading towards the reef. Other canoes were on their way. In one of them a young man was standing, poling himself along with his spear, its barbed head pointing upwards. At one moment as he was pressing on the spear, deep in the water behind him, he saw a fish ahead. Unhurriedly, without even altering his stance, he lifted the spear from the water, carried it over his head in the arc of a circle, and hurled it forward, all in a single movement. Then, sitting down, he paddled leisurely to where, a dozen yards ahead, the spear was threshing in the water with its impaled burden.

The power of balance of these people is astonishing. In the most precarious of craft, in rough water, they will stand and gaze about, as nonchalantly as if they were on a pier head. Many of the canoes are not more than nine or ten inches wide, their out-riggers scarce thicker than one's wrist. On horseback they have the same easiness of poise. Even small children, with only a halter for bridle, will ride bareback, at full gallop, over the roughest tracks.

Lauvi had to attend another council of chiefs, and was unable to go fishing. But two young men called for me, and accompanied by Charlie we set out in two canoes.

For the most part, near the shore, the floor of the lagoon was of clear sand, but further away there were increasing numbers of patches of 'stag's horn' coral, dense thickets of branching antlers, normally as safe for a fish as a blackthorn bush for a bird. But on this occasion the fish had little chance of escape. Each clump of coral was surrounded in turn. Baskets filled with twigs of coral were set at one end, and then from the other end there was a concerted drive of men and women, probing and thrusting with poles and spears. Forced to take cover in the camouflaged baskets, the fish were soon lifted to the surface and tipped into the canoes. Meanwhile, among the more massive formations of coral, men wearing goggles and armed with catapults were swimming under water. Fish seen lurking in crevices or sheltering under ledges were soon transfixed with an arrow that had once been the rib of an umbrella or the spoke of a bicycle wheel.

Floating on the surface I could watch these men through my goggles, as they glided from rock to rock, weightless, moving without effort, under a ceiling of shimmering crystal. Parrot fish of purple and cobalt blue, squirrel fish of crimson and gold, surgeon fish black as mourning *crêpe*, and trigger fish of many hues, soon joined the host of smaller victims.

As the sun drew near to the sea, strange dripping figures came ashore; men like tritons, women like sea crones, their hair soaked and tangled, as in a legend of amphibious creatures.

For several days after this the weather was perfect, clear cloudless skies and a gentle wind rippling the surface of the lagoon. I wandered about, watching the people at their daily avocations. Those who say that the Samoans are lazy should live among them for a while in a village, not in the town. From the first moment of dawn figures begin to move about on the *malae*. The Samoan will have done a couple of hours' work before the European is awake. At night, when the European is relaxing or asleep, many Samoans will be on the reef or in canoes, fishing. It is true that during the heat of the day many able-bodied men may be seen 'idle' in their *fales*, but if one could look into European houses as easily as into Samoan *fales* there might be seen just as many people taking their siesta, with perhaps less justification. If the Samoan led the life that romantic books and films suggest, he could not have the superb physical development that makes even an athlete from other countries look a weakling beside him. In Sa'anapu a man thought nothing of carrying more than a hundredweight of bananas and taro on a pole across his shoulders, for a distance of four miles. He said it was an average load. An eleven-year-old boy carried half that weight with as little thought. There may not be much working to the clock in Samoa, but there is plenty of work.

There was always something to watch in the village, if it was only a man weaving an eye-shade from a fragment of palm frond, or another making fire with two sticks, or a couple of youths preparing the daily oven, or women grating arrowroot, or, among the nobler callings, men building a house.

A box of matches is a rarity in Sa'anapu. Instead of being dependent for them on a store several miles away, it is so much easier to rub two sticks against each other. One is held flat on the ground with the foot, the other is held in the hands and rubbed backwards and forwards, at an angle, along the piece that lies on the ground. As this is done, a groove is formed in the lower unit and small particles of displaced wood accumulate there. Provided the wood is dry and the friction steadily increased, those particles soon begin to smoulder, and with the addition of a little tinder can be quickly blown into a flame. It is only necessary for the effort to be made once each day in the village. Torches carried from house to house supply the needs of all.

The oven, or *umu*, a shallow pit in the floor of the cook-house, is usually prepared by the young men of a family. Scraping out the ashes of the last day's fire, they put in sufficient timber to ensure a thorough heating of the stones which are to be heaped on top. Meanwhile, the women are getting the food ready for cooking, and when, eventually, the fire dies down the red-hot stones are raked aside to form a hollow in which the packages of food are placed; chickens, fish, vegetables, all at the same time, and each in its own wrapping of leaves. Those that require most heat, like taro and green bananas, are put in direct contact with the stones; others more sensitive, such as the small fish, are kept further away. When all are in place, they are covered with layer after layer of breadfruit and banana leaves, and left for about an hour, by which time they are ready for the food mat.

It is true that large pigs may need more than an hour in the oven, even when their interiors have been filled with hot stones, but it is not customary to serve large pigs fully cooked. In order to achieve the necessary precision in the ceremonial division of such an animal, it is almost essential that it should be carved when in an undercooked condition —flesh that fell too easily from the bones might lead to recriminations. Recipients are not expected to partake of the flesh where and when it is received; on the contrary, it is sent to their homes, and in due course recooked for a subsequent meal. Those unacquainted with this custom might think that Samoans like raw pork. This is not true. But I can't say that the sight of it being dismembered, during a meal, adds to one's appetite.

The *umu* is the regular method of cooking in all the Polynesian islands, even on the atolls where the necessary basaltic stones have to be imported. Coral is useless for the purpose, as it will not stand the heat and soon crumbles away.

Near to the cookhouse, while the oven is in preparation, a girl may be seen sitting astride a low three-legged trestle fitted in front with a narrow metal blade. On this she will be scraping the flesh of coco-nuts into fine shreds from which, later, by wringing through fibres, she will express the cream. This cream will be poured into cups formed of several thicknesses of taro leaves, and these, deftly closed and wrapped in other leaves, will be added to the oven. When cooked, the combined leaves and cream are known as *palusami*, one of the most favoured vegetable foods. Coco-nut cream is an all-important ingredient in Samoan cookery. In my own opinion, no cow ever produced a better addition to fruit or coffee.

On my last evening in the village I was taken across the *malae* to the house of Anapu, the high chief, from whom the village takes its name. The young men were giving a *fiafia*, a 'make happy,' in my honour. Anapu was away from home, but Lauvi and one or two other chiefs were there awaiting me. The big *fale* looked high, wide, and empty when I entered, and before my hosts appeared I had time to admire the construction of the roof, a vista of inter-secting beams reaching, in many tiers, high into the dark dome. There are no nails in Samoan house construction, and little morticing. Timbers are bound together with sennit, woven into intricate and decorative patterns.

Very soon the young men, 'the strength of the village' as they are called, began to arrive, and the side of the *fale* on my left was crowded with seated figures—dark bodies glossy as chestnuts, with brightly coloured *lavalavas* about their hips. No young woman was present; only a few children and their elders. In the more conservative districts of which Sa'anapu is a notable example—they do not even allow a trading store in the village—there is still the ancient disapproval of young men and maidens of the same village meeting for any form of hilarity. All the gaiety of mixed company comes about when parties of either sex visit other villages.

Each young man had brought with him a basket of food, and now one of their number came forward. As each basket was handed to him by an assistant, he took out the contents, announced what they were, and laid them in heaps

72

according to their kind, on the mats before me. Each basket contained drinking nuts, leaf packages of cooked fish, *palusami*, and baked taro. Rapidly the food was laid out, the servers moving swiftly and silently, always bending slightly, out of deference to the presence of chiefs. Now and then a nut rolled away and was retrieved from among the guests; sometimes a fish slipped out of the bread-fruit leaf that wrapped it and slid on to the floor. The pile of pale, husked nuts rose high beside the heap of leafy packages and the massed taro. At length the last basket was emptied, the final nut added to the pile, and I made my speech of thanks, handing over as my contribution to the feast a six-pound tin of *pisupo*. Then the food was portioned out according to 'my' instructions—the routine baskets for the *faifeau*, the doctor, chiefs, and *taupou*, some to take away with me the next day, and the rest divided among the guests.

The feast began. I sat cross-legged before my laden food mat, and regretted the meal I had so recently consumed in my *fale*. Surreptitiously, at intervals, I slipped hunks of taro and limbs of chickens to the small figures who clustered expectantly outside the house. Even that made little impression on the abundance before me. But if I lacked appetite, there was no such deficiency among the rest of the gathering; the young men wasted no time on conversation, but with surprising speed demolished the food which was piled before them. Coco-nuts were supplied for drinking, and as each one finished his meal a bowl of water and a cloth were brought for him to wash his hands. Soon all signs of the feast had disappeared, mats and baskets had been whisked out of sight, and the young men also disappeared to prepare themselves for the dancing. Little girls picked up bits of leaves and scraps of food from the floor, Lauvi sat rolling sennit, and I sat back and waited.

It was some time before the young men returned. When they did come back they entered at the far end of the *fale*. Those who were to form the orchestra sat in a group, two of them with rolls of mat on which they would beat the rhythm with sticks; the others would sing. It was quite dark outside. Beyond the light thrown from the *fale* one could distinguish the figures of girls, peering from a seemly distance.

Songs came first on the programme. The leader stood in the middle of the group, and in a high, clear voice announced the opening phrase of each verse. Then the drums would take up the rhythm and the other voices join in, in rich full harmonies.

After three songs there was a pause. Then, suddenly, as the music started again, a figure in a crimson *lavalava* leapt from the outside darkness. His arms and torso shone with oil, an *ula* of green banana leaves hung around his neck, bracelets of leaves were on his wrists and anklets about his feet. He stood a moment on the long mat which had been spread on the white coral floor, held out his hands in a swift gesture of greeting, and then began to dance; quietly at first, but with increasing vigour, often with his hands beating a syncopated tattoo on his bare arms and torso, often with gestures whose significance brought a shout of appreciative laughter from the onlookers. Two other men joined him, one on either side though always in the background, emphasizing his movements by their own, at times clowning to enhance his agility. Perfect rhythm, perfect muscular control; movements like steel springs uncoiling. As dancer succeeded dancer the tempo varied. Sometimes there would be hardly more than a delicate movement of arms and hands; at others, a fierce, wild distortion of limbs and body as in exultant abandon the dancer leapt high into the air.

That was to be my last evening in the village. Before going to bed I walked awhile beside the lagoon. The tide was low, the water bejewelled with phosphorescent light. Every footstep at the water's edge brought a glory to the sand.

CHAPTER ELEVEN

ONE MORNING AT MALUA, about twelve miles to the west of Apia, I was wandering in the bush, hoping to catch a glimpse of a tooth-billed pigeon. Instead of the usual type of bill of other doves, this bird has a heavy beak almost like that of a parrot, but with the upper mandible notched, suggesting teeth. Nowhere else in the world but in Samoa is it to be found, and in Samoa it is rare. My luck was out. I saw fan-tail fly-catchers high up among the giant pods of hanging vines, their outspread tails translucent in the sunlight. I saw a grey owl that might have been a barn owl from England. I saw small green parakeets, doves, banded rails, swamp hens, and numbers of black-bellied honey-suckers with their brilliant scarlet heads. But, high or low, there was no hint of the dark-green head or the rich chestnut body of the tooth-billed pigeon.

Returning towards the village, I noticed two young men high up among the many branches of a banyan-tree. They were slicing at the stems with knives, and as white juice

75

exuded from the cuts they smeared it on to stiff laurel-like leaves which they had gathered from another tree. These they then let fall to the ground: there must have been a couple of hundred of them patterning the earth at the foot of the tree. For a while I watched them moving among the branches, the broken sunlight dappling their lissom bodies, then, as I began to move homeward, the two boys slipped nimbly to the ground and began to gather up the leaves.

'Kirikiti,' said one, in answer to my halting inquiry.

'Clicket,' said the other. '*Polo* clicket.'

The word *polo* means ball, and may be derived from the English word, the 'b' and the 'p' being interchanged and a final vowel added; but, like many Polynesian words, it may have come from Indonesia—a fact used in the argument that the Polynesian people had their origin at least as far west as Malay. The English derive their word 'polo' from the Tibetan name for the game, *pulu*, though it was in Persia that polo appears to have originated, records of it being played there going back as far as 600 B.C. Indeed, there seems every indication that Darius the king, whose law altered not, indulged in an occasional chukka when not throwing people to the lions. Twelve centuries later, Harun-al-Rashid was so small when he began to play that he could scarcely reach the ball with his polo stick; and in the tale of King Yunan and the doctor, in *The Arabian Nights*, we are told how the physician cured the king of leprosy by inserting various herbs into the head of a polo stick which he had carved for the purpose and then prescribing that the king should 'ride on his horse to the polo ground and there exercise with the mallet and ball.' According as the king became warm and the pores of the skin on his hand became open, so he would absorb the medicine. And it happened even as the physician had predicted, for the king's skin became 'pure and stainless as virgin silver.' Incidentally, the doctor became the richer by three thousand dinars and many robes of honour.

But the Samoans do not vex their heads with countries

of origin either of their games or of themselves. 'The rest of the Polynesians may have come from Asia,' they say, 'but not the Samoans. No, the Samoans originated in Samoa.' *Sa* means sacred, *moa* means centre. Sa-moa means 'sacred centre of the earth.' Like all other nations of the world they believe that they are the elect of the Creator. They speak of themselves as *toto moni*, of true blood; of others as *toto leanga*, of common blood. Like all other peoples, they believe that their way of life is the best because, like all other peoples, they judge only by their own standards.

Soon after I got back to the village I found one of the boys sitting under a tree with the leaves spread around him. The white juice had dried to a colourless film, and he was peeling this adhesive skin from the leaves and winding it, layer after layer, on to a core of the same material, a lump of coagulated juice which he had brought with him from an earlier wound in the tree. Soon the ball was completed. Its form was not mathematically correct, but it was a reasonable sphere of natural rubber, hard and ready for immediate use. He said that he would take it with him that afternoon when he went to play at a neighbouring village. In this connection it is interesting to note that the thousands of rubber balls which the Aztecs demanded as a yearly tribute from their subjugated tribes, and which they used in their stadiums, were probably made in a similar way from unrefined natural rubber.

I understand that at Lord's, in Middlesex, England, they have set rules for cricket. This, I think, is a mistake. It is a much better game as played in Samoa. For instance, at Lord's not more than eleven players may take part on either side; in Samoa there is no such limitation, teams can have forty, seventy, a hundred, or as many as wish to play. Neither do the Samoans worry if the teams are unequal in numbers: after all, the purpose of the play is to win the match, and the side that can put most players into the field stands the better chance. One feature of the game in

England that might well be altered is the continual changing of the whole field after every six balls. In Samoa there is none of that. They just bowl from whichever end the ball happens to be. It saves a vast amount of time. Critics might say: 'What about the fielding?' But with a hundred men in the field it is perfectly easy to arrange for all eventualities. Actually, hitting is pretty straightforward; none of that over-precious cutting to slips, or tiresome leg glides. When it is understood that the batsman makes a good, honest slog at every ball, whether it be a full pitch bowled overarm or a low bouncer bowled underarm, it simplifies the whole problem of fielding. Whereas in England, in matter of speed, cricket competes with chess, in Samoa, both in speed and entertainment, it is more like a non-stop revue. Bowling is continuous. Even when a batsman is out the bowler continues his deliveries, and if the next batsman is not there to defend his wicket and it is hit, then he is out before he is in. For that reason two or three batsmen sit at the position known in England as point, ready to leap to the wicket the moment it goes down. Runs are very wearisome to a batsman: when he has rushed up and down the pitch several times in quick succession he cannot possibly be in a fit state to 'make a good strike.' In Samoa they provide runners. Two stand at each end, beside an auxiliary wicket, each with a stick in his hand. It is really a kind of relay race affiliated to cricket, but it does leave the batsman free for his job.

There are many other ideas that impressed me. For instance, it might add to the interest of the game in England, particularly in county cricket, if the home team had the right to make a new rule on the eve of the fixture without any obligation to inform the visitors until occasion arose in the course of the game. In Samoa that often helps to dispose of a troublesome batsman. Then, again, a cheer-leader would lighten the tedium of an afternoon's play. In Samoa he fields at mid-on and leads the applause, all the other fielders taking their cue from him. On the dismissal of a batsman at Lord's, it would enliven the scene if the whole team of fielders, augmented as I have suggested, turned cartwheels in unison or, alternatively, rolled a few times on the ground. And instead of just lounging in the pavilion I would like to see those batsmen not in play formed up as a choir, singing under their leader, with perhaps three or four of their number doing a step dance to the accompaniment of the singing—a very practical way of reviving folk dancing. In Samoa the choir-master carries a stick with which he wakens any member of his team whose energies may be flagging. It keeps the team 'on its toes,' even though they are sitting. And while on the subject of music, I might mention that a fielder with a couple of sticks and an old kerosene tin can keep up a tattoo of the greatest stimulus to the players. He can always leap to his feet and field a ball if it happens to come in his direction. In short, if the M.C.C. would link up with the ballet, there would be no more calls for brighter cricket. But it might be as well to mention as a warning that when cricket was first introduced into Samoa in 1885 by the officers and crew of H.M.S. *Diamond*, it took such a hold on the people that they abandoned all work on their plantations until, by order of the Church, the game was banned. I happened to be spending Christmas and the New Year in the village of Fangamalo, and for a fortnight, Sundays excepted, there was continuous cricket, mornings and afternoons. From my house I could see three different games in progress— men's teams on my left, women's in front, and children's to my right. The enthusiasm never waned. There was a constant noise of shrieking and laughter. Even a veritable deluge of rain did not deter the players. A few of the women held umbrellas over their heads when fielding, otherwise the players abandoned themselves to the rigours of the game. Women are keen exponents, not only in Samoa but on other islands. It is told that when a schooner was wrecked on Palmerston atoll the crew clambered ashore, expecting to have to fight 'the savages' for their lives. But, instead, they were challenged to a cricket match by the women of the island—and beaten.

Later in the year I was at Saluafata, a village some fifteen miles to the east of Apia, for the opening of a new pitch. This was a really important occasion, and there was much formality. Players and their supporters had arrived from all over the island. Thirty teams had entered for the contest, this time with the strict limit of twelve players. In all there must have been two thousand people gathered for the festival. On the first day the food distributed amounted to sixteen thousand taro roots, fifteen hundred double loaves of bread, twenty-two cattle, a hundred and ninety large pigs—the small pigs, like the ducks and chickens, were not considered worth counting—besides innumerable tins of *pisupo* and fish. The visiting teams had subscribed £800 towards the cost of the entertainment, but Tangaloa, the high chief of Saluafata, had had to make all the arrangements not only for the catering but for the housing of the multitude.

The whole of the opening day was given up to an elaborate pageantry of warriors marching and *taupous* dancing and clowns fooling, with vast presentations of food and much speech-making, praying, and hymn singing, against a background of flags and banners and decorated *fales* that might have been the pavilions of medieval knights. Bulls led in for sacrifice by young men whose heads were wreathed in flowers and whose bare shoulders glistened with oil, carried the imagination even further back in history.

The pitch had been decorated with flowers. Coloured ribbons at each end of it awaited the ceremonial knife. Teams marched about the *malae*, each bearing its own standard, each with its own title: 'The Forbidden Fish' came from the village of Luatuanu'u, 'The Sacred Cave' from Sa'anapu, 'The Nine-headed Pigeon' from Poutasi, 'The Pearl' from Savaia, and 'The Ripe Orange' from Vaie'e. But it was not until after midday that the actual opening ceremony was performed by two of the captains. With each ribbon severed, two rifle shots were fired. Then group after group of men from the various villages marched on to the *malae* and sat, in squares, around the pitch. A master of ceremonies took command, and from then till close on midnight there was a continuous entertainment of song and dance. The tournament began next morning, and continued for ten days. Any team that was beaten could compete again by payment of another entrance fee. The tourney only finished when funds and food were exhausted.

As from the cricket ground I heard the galloping of ponies backwards and forwards on the nearby road, I could not help thinking what a fine game polo might be if introduced into Samoa. With ponies, of which there are plenty, ridden bareback, without a bridle, with an unlimited number of players on either side, and a ground far from level, there should be plenty of that 'speed' for which the game is famous. There need be no difficulty about equipment: when the 10th Hussars introduced the game to England in 1869 they played with crooked sticks and a billiard ball. And if, as with Samoan cricket, there should be music to encourage the players, that will be in the best tradition: an illustration in an early Persian manuscript shows an orchestra of drummers playing while a game is in progress.

CHAPTER TWELVE

I FOUND LITTLE COMFORT in Apia until I found 'Tina's.' Then I found luxury; a large room for a study, with a bedroom adjoining, and both of them opening on to a balcony from which I could look across the harbour to the town and its encircling hills. Frank, the only other lodger in the house, was working for an examination and was also in love, 'either of them enough to keep a man quiet.'

'You won't be disturbed. I'll see to that,' said Tina; and she did.

Instead of being a headquarters, the house very soon became a home. Whether I got back early or late from an expedition there was always a welcome. 'Come in, come in! Did you have a good trip? I made a lemon pie for lunch, I thought you'd be back, but I saved a piece for your dinner. And I've got you a bottle—on lease-lend from Frank. I said, Frank, that man's coming back to-day, I must have something for him. Are you hot now? Do you want a shower before your tea? Mind the paint in the bathroom, it's wet. There was a man in here asking for you, a Major somebody—said he met you in Fiji. I said you were a busy man, couldn't see anybody. And that girl in the store, she came round wanting you to make a picture of her. I said you go along get your photo taken, Mr. Gibbings got no time for that, he's working hard on his book. I've taken the chair out of Frank's room for you; he doesn't need it. You can have another pillow from his bed, too, if you like—he won't miss it.'

Although Tina was strict with casual callers, established friends had no difficulty in finding me. Usually I had warning of their approach from Tina's conversation shouted to them as they mounted the stairs. 'Mind yourself on the back balcony; Frank's got Nancy's bicycle up there. She left it on the road where the truck would go over it.' Or: 'Have you got any eggs at Mulifanua? I must have some. Mr. Gibbings likes them for his sandwiches.' Or: 'Why didn't you come in the daylight? I could have shown you my new banana plants.'

One day Captain Matheson of the schooner *Tagua* came to see me. They were sailing for the Tokelau Islands next day, he said, and there was a spare bunk on board. Would I care to come? The doctor would be coming too, on a tour of inspection, and there was a chap called Deasy, a trader, who wanted to have a look around. We would have a day or two at each of the three islands while they were putting stores ashore and taking copra on board. He suggested that I should bring with me any old shirts that I could spare, or a few lengths of cotton or some bars of soap, to trade for mats—'the best mats in the Islands,' he said.

So the following afternoon I was on board the schooner, and we were heading north for the Tokelaus, three hundred miles away. Nothing to do but sit in the shade of the mainsail, watch the sea go by, and listen to the chief engineer or Sparks, the radio operator, or Deasy, spinning yarns and arguing.

Deasy, who comes from Donegal, has been in the Islands for twenty years. 'Disi,' the natives call him. His fair skin has never got used to the tropical sun and is constantly peeling, and his shock of red hair has never got used to discipline and is always in revolt. He is lean and active, ever ready to turn his hand to anything, but restless, never able to stay long in one place.

'I 'm a rolling stone,' he said, 'and I 'm gathering little moss; I 'm not even getting a polish.'

'You 're Irish and you 're just like the Samoans. You don't care much for hard work, you 'd rather sit about and talk,' said the chief engineer. He and Deasy were old friends.

'And may I ask,' said Deasy, 'why you 're sweating your soul out in the engine-room day after day? Isn't it only to earn enough to retire on and do damn all ever after?'

'The Samoans are the Irish of the Pacific. They 're always agin the Government,' said the chief.

Deasy stretched his hands above his head as if to claw down chunks of atmosphere. 'Isn't every country in the world agin a government that isn't its own? Isn't every patriot a rebel to the other side?'

'Let 's talk about love,' said Sparks.

'In the Cook Islands,' said the doctor, 'there 's a curfew at nine o'clock every night. Any one found out of doors after that is fined. It isn't so very long since any young couple walking together after dusk had to carry a lighted torch between them, just to show they weren't holding hands. Yes, and if a man was seen to cry over a dead woman that wasn't an immediate relation of his he was hauled off to the court and fined.'

The three islands of the Tokelau group, Fakaofu, Nuku-nono, and Atafu, to which we were sailing, suffered grievously from slave-raiders during the latter half of the nineteenth century. Between the years 1850 and 1870, and in particular during the period from 1862 to 1864, the islands were raided by ships from South America, 'black-birding' for the guano islands and sugar plantations of

Peru. The population was almost exterminated. A native teacher, resident at that time on Atafu, wrote: 'This is my letter. Our country is destroyed. All our people have been carried away in a foreign ship. They were deceived by offers of trading. The captain told them to take off to the ship coco-nuts and fowls to sell, and he brought forth some cloth and a shirt and trousers, and said to the men, bring your coco-nuts and fowls to buy these things. Then I said, come on shore and purchase. The captain replied, I don't wish to purchase ashore; it will be better to buy aboard. . . . All the people of this island are carried off. They have taken the chief, Oli, who was in Samoa, and thirty-four other men. All that now remain here are women and children, and six male adults. Sir, it is most piteous to witness the grief of these women and children. They are weeping night and day; they do not eat, there is none left to provide food for them, or to climb the coco-nut trees. They will perish with hunger.'

At about the same time two hundred and forty-seven men, women, and children were kidnapped from Fakaofu, of whom only one ever returned; 'many of the women far advanced in pregnancy, others with children at the breast.' Only eighty inhabitants out of several hundred were left on Nukunono. It was a widespread traffic. From Nukulaelae in the Ellice group, five hundred miles to the west, they captured nearly three hundred out of a population of about four hundred. Not one ever returned. From Penrhyn, eight hundred miles to the east, they took close on a thousand, most of whom died away from home. From Pukapuka they took about a hundred, of whom only one saw home again. Easter Island, four thousand miles to the south-east, and others not so far away, Niue, Manihiki, Mangaia, all suffered in the same way.

But the only things that we hoped to take from the islands were spiders, rats, and mats. The doctor wanted all the spiders he could collect for a museum in New Zealand; he wanted to inspect the rats for fleas, which are carriers of plague, for the sake of the islanders; and we

85

both wanted mats for the sake of our floors. Meanwhile, having arrived, we had to get ashore.

The Tokelau canoes are very much bigger than the craft one sees in Samoa, many of them being up to forty feet in length—in the olden times still longer. Nevertheless, they do not inspire any great confidence. The bottom of the hull is composed of sections of a hollowed tree which meet, end to end, without morticing, and are held together with lashings of sennit. The sides are a built-up patchwork of many irregular scraps of wood shaped to fit each other, and, like the sections of the keel, sewn together with sennit— a technique evolved owing to the scarcity of large trees on the atolls. One's emotions are mixed when, a mile from the shore, with only a few inches of freeboard and a thousand fathoms of water below, one watches fountains of water pouring through the holes only partly filled by the stitching. But the Tokelau bailer is shaped to fit the inside

curve of the canoe, and the flood of events is to some extent controlled. The reef is wide, and successive lines of waves surge in obliquely. If, now, they are charging from the right, a moment later there will be a broadside from the left. Only by constant quick changes of direction were we able to reach calm water and wade towards the glare of the white sand, forgetting the glare of the sea.

Fakaofu is an atoll of sixty islets surrounding a lagoon, triangular in shape, about seven miles in length and five at its greatest width. The average height of the land above sea level is not more than a dozen feet. The whole population, of close on six hundred, lives in an overcrowded condition on one islet—so overcrowded that piers have been built into the lagoon to give further ground space for houses. Many of the other islets would be equally suitable for habitation, but there is rivalry between Protestant and Catholic congregations, and each needs all its adherents close at hand. They still remember that one of their high chiefs was killed in a war between champions of the two creeds.

But the village is a model of town planning, with roads and paths carefully laid out and edged with stone. Even the chickens have their appointed roosts. Though free to roam during the day, each one returns at night to its own perch, set up over a rectangle of sand and edged with stones like the road.

No sooner were we ashore than it seemed to the crowd of inquisitive children who had surrounded us that the doctor was showing signs of lunacy. Pointing to the sky, he appeared to be offering cigarettes to any child who would go there. His audience was bewildered. At first they thought he was being playful for their benefit, and crowded round him; but, with further and more excited gesticulations on his part, they thought he was mad, and edged away. Just then the policeman appeared in sight. 'Come quickly,' shouted the doctor, 'come quickly! Tell them I want that spider. There it is—hanging from that breadfruit leaf, about two feet down.'

The children burst out laughing. The chiefs who had gathered to watch became solemn, as if anxious. This was the official who had come to inspect their health. But a boy went up the tree, and with a long wand entangled the web and brought the spider to earth.

'Tell them,' said the doctor, 'that I'll give a cigarette for every spider they bring me.'

The children were incredulous.

'And tell them,' he added, 'that I'll give two cigarettes for every rat they bring me.' This was too much even for the composure of the chiefs. They, too, burst out laughing. 'I want to see what fleas they are carrying,' said the doctor. That was funnier still. And because I had come ashore with the doctor, and because I seemed to understand what he was doing, I was classed as a potential lunatic. I couldn't move without being followed by a crowd of hopeful children. If I stopped to look at one of the long

87

poles, forked at the end, with which they twist the bread-fruit from the upper branches of the trees; or if I paused beside a house to look at the clusters of empty coco-nuts strung on sennit with which they draw water from their wells; or if I watched an old woman husking coco-nuts on an iron spike stuck in the ground; 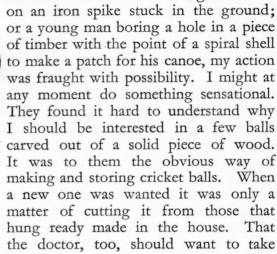 or a young man boring a hole in a piece of timber with the point of a spiral shell to make a patch for his canoe, my action was fraught with possibility. I might at any moment do something sensational. They found it hard to understand why I should be interested in a few balls carved out of a solid piece of wood. It was to them the obvious way of making and storing cricket balls. When a new one was wanted it was only a matter of cutting it from those that hung ready made in the house. That the doctor, too, should want to take away such commonplace things as fish-hooks and paddles, not to mention the wooden buckets with water-tight lids in which fishermen carry their food when at sea, was altogether astonishing.

At Fakaofu mats were scarce, but at Nukunono we found profusion of them. Everything that we had taken with us for barter was soon exchanged; we had difficulty in retaining the shirts on our backs. From Atafu we came away laden with presents of fans and shell necklaces.

The voyage home was calm and uneventful, the schooner riding kindly to the long, gentle swell.

Deasy told us how, when living in the Cook Islands, he had fallen in love with a chief's daughter. 'I'd have married her,' he said, 'if I'd been free, but I wasn't—the same old story, never mind! I spoke to the chief about it, and he told her to come along. So she came along, and we were as happy as skylarks in May. She helped me in the store and I taught her a bit of cooking. Next thing the pastor and deacons have me up before the Resident Agent, and I'm fined eight shillings and she's fined two shillings for misdemeanour. "Divil take the lot of you," said I, "'tis you'll pay those fines and not me." And they did, though they didn't know it. I put a penny extra on everything they bought until they'd worked them off.'

Tina gave me her usual welcome. 'Come in, come in! Did you have a good trip? Wait while I telephone—Granny saw you coming. Hallo! Exchange? Put me on to Mata again. What? No, you didn't! You cut me off, and I haven't got my eggs. I must have—what? Hallo! Hallo! Who's that? What! Is that you, Tomi? Where's Mata? You don't know? Well, what about those eggs? I must have them. I must have eggs for Mr. Gibbings's tea. You what? You don't know where to find them? Why, in the nests, of course. They don't lay in the palms. No, in the morning won't do. You go out and have a look right now. I'm sending Elva round for them.'

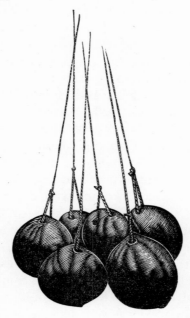

CHAPTER THIRTEEN

THERE WAS DISAPPOINTMENT in Fangamalo when the governor was unable to pay his expected visit to the village. While on a tour of Savai'i, some urgent duty had recalled him to Upolu. All the preparations had been for nought. But the children upheld the principle that half a pig is better than no pork, and on the morning after my arrival on the island I received an invitation to visit the school. So along I went, to find flags flying, children and teachers paraded. The programme that had been prepared for the governor was to be worked off on me.

The first item was a song of welcome, shrill and strident, sung *fortissimo*. This was followed by a *siva*, and then came the Lord's Prayer, not quite so *forte*. There followed a medley of dances and hymns, songs and prayers. Throughout the *sivas* the children in the front row, who looked scarcely more than three years old, were twitching with excitement. It needed only the slightest hint on my part for a dozen of them to leap to their feet. Then I really did see the *siva*, in its most spontaneous expression.

Even before they can walk, Samoan children learn to dance. Babies in their mothers' arms, looking on while others *siva*, wave and clap their hands in time with the music; tiny children, swaying on unsteady feet, posture and wriggle to the rhythm of the drums. Many a time, when grown-up men and women were dancing, I have seen children edging in from the outskirts of the *fale*, intent on every movement of their elders, hardly able to restrain their own desire for action.

Before I left the school I was shown some of the books from which the elder children were learning English, and my eye chanced on this: 'Robert Louis Stevenson, who was born in Scotland, was too delicate to do hard work;

instead, he became a writer of books.' Somehow the sentence stuck in my memory.

My temporary home was in a wooden building formerly 'The Residency' of the island, and Joane, the local policeman, was my host.

Fa'aniniva, his wife, was very proud of her five children, five out of the eighteen of whom Joane was the father. 'First woman, she have one baby, that baby live, the woman die,' said Fa'aniniva. 'Second woman, she have eight children, all die only one. Woman die, too. Third woman she have four, only two live. That woman die. Fourth woman, that me, she have five children—all live, all strong, all very strong. My babies they all live.'

I had hardly been in the house an hour when Joane asked if they might call the last of those babies, a boy of a week old, after me. They would like to call him Kipingi, he said. In the Samoan language there are only nine consonants, and 'g' always has the sound of 'ng,' as in singer. The nearest they can get to the hard 'g' is our 'k,' which, though not actually in their language, is used in words of foreign origin. Neither have they a 'b'; that becomes 'p.' And so, as all words end in a vowel, my name became Kipingi.

But little Kipingi was not the first child to derive its name from my visit to Samoa. At various villages where I had stayed two boys had been called Lopati (Robert), another had been called Tusitala, and a girl was named Aialani because her mother heard that I came from Ireland.

Joane had acquired his knowledge of English from a friend who had been in the New Hebrides, so that at times there was a touch of 'beach-la-mar'—the trade jargon of those western isles—in his voice. He was a very busy man: his duties must have taken up a full hour of his time every day. And just when I arrived he was particularly worried by the prisoner who had been allotted to him for labour. 'This plisoner no good. He not work. Lazy, lazy! Sleep all time. Next week we get nice new plisoner, velly nice new plisoner. Me tired. Too much work!'

D

That morning the work had been to interview a man whose pig he had shot. Though it is against the law in Samoa for pigs to be kept near the houses, there are few villages in which a pig may not be seen roaming. Occasionally the edict is sent forth that any of these animals seen in a village are to be shot by the local constable. 'Last week I shoot pig,' said Joane. '*Kovana* (governor) say shoot all pig in village. I shoot pig. To-day man belong pig come along, he say he velly solly. He say him no fault, he say me no fault; he say just pig he make mistake.'

All the time music. From the early hours of dawn the notes of a guitar or ukulele coming from a *fale*, or from youth or maid who, passing, touches lightly on the strings. Even a mother while suckling her baby will play softly on her guitar; even a child picking his steps towards the 'little house' that stands in the lagoon will tinkle as he goes, will tinkle also while he sits.

Most of these instruments are home-made; the half-shell of a coco-nut gives pleasant tone as a sound-box, an empty pilchard tin gives a more metallic note. It is not generally known that the word ukulele was originally a nickname for a sprightly young Englishman who, about the year 1879, was chamberlain to the jovial King Kalakaua of Hawaii. In contrast to the king, who was heavy and stately, this young man was extremely agile in his movements, so much so that he became known, affectionately, as 'jumping flea'—in Hawaiian *uku lele*. Because he was rarely seen without one of the small guitars that at that time were being introduced from Portugal, those instruments acquired the same name.

There is great peace at Fangamalo. Save for the music, an occasional murmur of human voices, and the far rustle of the reef, there is no sound. Only at rare intervals does one hear the drums, the big *lali* to summon the people to

church, the smaller hand drums to call the children to school. And everywhere a glow of colour, colour that is alive and changing. At one moment the hibiscus flowers are a vivid crimson, at the next a scarlet, bright as flame. The swathes of lilies on the lawns are the colours of hydrangeas, blue or pink according to the light. Day after day the lagoon shimmers, a moonstone blue.

At almost any hour of the day there are fishermen in the lagoon. It may be a solitary youth with a throw-net in the shallow water; or it may be men, far out on the reef, hurling their spears into the on-coming waves. Sometimes in the early morning there is a procession of canoes: singly or by twos or threes they pass. At a given point they will deploy, closing in again, later, to form a circle. Inside that circle are heaped up coral rocks. The plan is

to drive the fish into the crevices of the coral and then to
swim down and spear them. At a signal from the head
fisherman, who blows a conch shell, every one beats the
side of his canoe with his paddle, making as much noise as
possible to frighten the fish. Another note from the conch
and every one goes overboard. From then on for half an
hour little is to be seen but empty canoes and an occasional
head or pair of feet momentarily above the water.

Another time one will see the *matais*, the heads of
families, holding conference, and one will be told that they
are planning a *lauloa*, a method of fishing in which a long
sweep of coco-nut fronds, strung on lianas, is dragged
through the water towards a waiting purse-net. Each
family in the village must provide a certain length of this
sweep—perhaps ten fathoms. Then, when all is ready and
the tide is right, men, women, and children will combine,
with shouting and splashing and laughter, to haul it
through the water, and, oftentimes, great is the harvest.

The only despoiler of my peace was Simi. He had
appropriated me from the first. I could not move outside my house without seeing him appear. He had spent
some years in Apia and could speak English, but his ideas
were limited. 'To-morrow morning I go church: after
church I find you nice girl.' He made the same proposi-
tion, in varying forms, almost daily. I began to think he
used it to fill in gaps in the conversation. He always
emphasized that he was of full Samoan blood, yet his
features suggested a strong Melanesian influence; indeed,
there were times when it seemed to me that an 'an'
added to his name might have given a truer hint of his
ancestry.

His capacity for jockeying his friends into my services
was unlimited, and equalled only by his skill in jockeying
me into situations from which a hand in the pocket was the
only means of escape. At last I got tired of it. I told
him that I was sick of his everlasting demands for money,
that already I was paying him more than double what he
would get elsewhere, and that in addition I had given him

endless presents. I said he could go, that I was through with his services.

But Simi didn't move. He stood as if waiting for me to go on talking.

'What are you waiting for?' I asked.

'Give me shilling for smokes,' he said.

But if Simi was exasperating, Joane was magnanimous. If I tried to make any return for his innumerable attentions he would look at me reproachfully. 'No, sar, no. Me Bri'sh, you Bri'sh.' Only once did the balance of imperial preference favour his side.

'Thank you velly much, Mr. Kipingi. I like velly much I owe you one pound and five chilling. I buy peeg, velly beeg peeg. I buy 'im last *Juni*. My family, twenty-six, all come village. I make 'em feast, beeg feast. All stomachs heavy. Beeg peeg, eight pound I pay. I say every month I give one pound. Last month I only have fifteen chilling. This day man write, say he want one pound and five chilling. Thank you velly much, Mr. Kipingi.'

In Samoa the laws of hospitality outweigh all other con-siderations. A man *must* do what is expected of him, no matter what the consequences. To fail in any detail brings not only immediate loss of personal prestige but shame and disgrace on his whole family. Many a man has stolen a pig and gone to prison, voluntarily, for the theft, rather than bring dishonour on his relations. There are times when he just has to have a pig. How he obtains it is a secondary consideration. And, of course, the higher the rank the bigger the pig. In an unpublished manuscript, the diary of William Oliver, yeoman, who left Devonshire about 1860 and spent most of his subsequent life in the Cook Islands, we read the results of marrying into a royal family:

'Queen Makea's mother is my oldest sister and her daughter is Queen Tinamana of Arorangi, and Queen Pa of Ngatangiia is my first cousin! . . . On April 17th, 1890 my wife's nephew Vairakau died. My fat pig died the same day, 300 pounds of pork gone for Royalty!

'On June 13th, 1892 the widow of Old Tupe, my wife's sister-in-law, died, aged seventy, and another fat pig, 200 pounds, also died for Royalty. Oh Lord, have mercy on us.

'On September 25th, 1892 my wife's sister died and my best pig was yielded up to Royalty—in God we trust!'

CHAPTER FOURTEEN

THAT SAME WILLIAM OLIVER to whom 1 have already referred has other items of interest in his diary. After talking of a slight embarrassment that overtook him in Sydney due to the nurse of the family with whom he was staying, 'a Lady and a Scholar and a Good Young Woman, twenty-six years old, full of fun, love and affection,' who 'would insist on nursing me after the Baby was gone to sleep,' he writes: 'I left Sydney for Melbourne and arrived on February the Nineteenth, 1865. But I had only a short stay there, for one morning, keeping my eye on the Newspapers, I read:

'WANTED.—A Single Man to take charge of an Island in the South Pacific. Apply Nicholson & Sons, Ship Brokers, Elizabeth St. 9 a.m.

'I was on hand in time. After praying to my Heavenly Father for His assistance in procuring the situation, and thanking Him for His past mercy unto me, I heard a whisper in my right ear—"You shall have it." I saw no one, but heard the Voice only and from that moment I felt confident.'

He then describes how he was chosen from a large number of applicants, and how he was taken to meet Captain Murphy of the barque *Envoy*, 'a fine new vessel of 500 tons.' Afterwards he signed articles, 'as Captain of Victoria Island,' before the shipping master. 'Then with orders to be on board by 4 p.m. March the eighth we drew a month's pay in advance and saw the sights of Melbourne.

'At the time appointed we was onboard and the Mate showed us our berths which was fixed up in the Traderoom. . . . The same evening Mr. Nicholson and an Old Gentleman came off with Captain Murphy and handed me letters, papers and cash, asking me to deliver a parcel to the London Missionary Society at Rarotonga and another to the ditto at Aitutaki.

'All right, Gentlemen! Weigh Anchor, Boys! Everything was ready in fifteen minutes. Shake hands with my Boss and the Mish. Goodbye and God bless you and we were off.'

They reached Rarotonga on 12th May, and a week later continued on their course for Victoria Island, calling at Aitutaki for a few hours on the way. The narrative continues: 'After a fortnight Captain Murphy said we were near and he sent a man aloft. At daylight next morning another sailor went aloft, but again no land. Murphy said we were now within five miles of the Island and as we had strong trade-winds the barque was scudding. About nine o'clock the Captain and Mate worked out the reckoning and declared we had sailed right over the place. There was thousands of birds hovering around. . . . We ploughed the ocean for a hundred miles in all directions, but no land to be seen. . . . Captain Murphy was a splendid Navigator, he could pick up an island correctly if it was marked right on the chart.'

Yet a few years earlier, I was told, a certain William Marsters had landed on that island, leaving there a party of men to work the guano. Eighteen months later he had called again and taken the men away because, in the meantime, his company had 'gone bust.' A year later, on behalf of a new company, he took another party of men to the island, but this time there was no sign of the place. They sailed right over the position of the island but saw no trace of land, only, as Oliver also mentioned, many sea birds hovering about.

'Marsters!' said Deasy, who was visiting Savai'i and had dropped in to see me at Fangamalo. 'Marsters! Four wives and a couple of assistants. Well, I suppose with that number of women about the place a man might make a mistake of a night. More than thirty children he had, and the half of them has had as many more. There must be five hundred of them in the Islands to-day. And they're grand sailors. Wherever there's a mast there's a Marsters, you might say. You'll find three of them on the *Tagua*, and Jimmy the bos'n on the *Tiare* is another. The old man died on Palmerston—he owned the island. Two of his wives came from Penrhyn, and 'twas the people of Penrhyn sent the missionary down to educate all his little heathens that was running around. But Marsters was a kind of a jealous man, and when the missionary, a young native teacher, landed on the island to teach the children, "You'll teach 'em through the stockade," he says. You see, the missionary had once been a friend of one of the wives—I forget which one—and Marsters didn't trust him, missionary or lay teacher or whatever he was. So he drove a half-circle of stakes into the ground at the end of his house, and he fixed a bit of a roof of thatch over it, and inside it all he put the missionary. And the only door into the cage was through Marsters's bedroom and Marsters had a lock on the door and he kept the key in his pocket. And there he kept the man for half a year, never letting him go outside without himself alongside of him. And all the time he was teaching the children through the fence. Then one day 'tis "Sail-ho!" and the *Messenger of Peace* arrives— no, I'm wrong, 'twas the *John Williams* was plying the trade then. So Marsters puts the missionary in a boat and starts to row him out to the ship, and the missionary couldn't sit still in the boat with the excitement that he had. And when he gets half-way to the ship, he jumps up in the boat and starts waving and shouting to his mates on the ship. And Marsters was raging mad, for he couldn't row the boat with the way the fellow was lepping about in the stern. All of a sudden Marsters jumps to one side of the thwart, the boat gives a lurch, and over goes the preacher. "Swim for it now," says Marsters, "and to hell with yourself and your education." And with that he rowed back to the shore.'

William, the first of the Marsters family to reach Polynesia, was born in Birmingham. As a young man he had gone to sea in a whaling ship, but later left that to seek his fortune in the California gold rush. With a little money collected there he arrived in the Pacific, and after a while of wandering among the Islands he reached Palmerston in 1860. Palmerston is an atoll, about four and a half miles in greatest length, lying two hundred and seventy miles north-west of Rarotonga, and Marsters came there, bringing with him a party of natives from Penrhyn to manage a *bêche-de-mer* industry which had recently been established. But it wasn't long before the business petered out. Its directors faded out, too, and the manager was left in peace as monarch of the island. There he reigned in patriarchal power until his death in 1906.

It was a custom on Palmerston that, when a man died, any children born into his family at about that time should be called by a name reminiscent in some way of his last illness and death. When old William lay dying one of his daughters-in-law was on her way to visit him. But *en route*, at Aitutaki, she gave birth to a son, and when she reached Palmerston the old man had died. She therefore christened the boy Aaron Too-late Seventy-eight Marsters, and Aaron Too-late is to-day the living proof that his grandfather was seventy-eight when he died.

The invention of this name and of others similar in style which are found to-day in Polynesia reminds us of the enthusiasm of the sixteenth-century puritans who gave their children such names as Sin-denye, Sory-for-sine, Hate-evill, Faint-not, and Help-on-high. Perhaps the zenith of their zeal was reached in a family whose surname was Barebone, and in which two brothers were entitled, respectively, Jesus-Christ-came-into-the-world-to-save Barebone, and If-Christ-had-not-died-for-thee-thou-hadst-been-damned Barebone. It is said of the latter that his friends growing tired of calling him by such a long name abbreviated it to the last word in the phrase and that he became known as Damned Barebone.

'I reckon the old man had a pretty good time,' said another of Marsters's grandsons to me. 'Each of his wives had a separate house, and they were all good friends. He'd go and visit them in turn. They wouldn't let us do that kind of thing nowadays.'

But if his wives were placid the elements were less accommodating. Again and again every house on his island was destroyed by hurricanes. Finally Marsters decided to put up a building that would withstand any storm. 'There never was another house like it,' said his grandson. The posts, six feet apart, were sunk fourteen feet into the sand and coral. They were two feet thick each way. The walls and the flooring were of baulks of wood eight and ten inches thick, held together with heavy iron bolts. The timber was from a lumber schooner that had been wrecked on the reef, and the bolts from another ship that had met a similar fate. 'Oh, plenty of wrecks; schooners, and barques,' said young Marsters. 'Many *motus* called after them—Spar Bank, Thistle Bank, Julia Cobb Bank.' And many a bit of iron beaten into a fish spear.

'And a queer thing,' said the grandson to me. 'The old man would know of a thing that had happened far away a long time before there was news of it. There was his daughter Marion who had been living in Rarotonga with her two daughters. One day a schooner came in that was going to Palmerston, and she thought she'd go and see her relations. So she and the children and a woman called Munokoa went on board. But one way and another the schooner got into difficulties, her steering gear broke, she had no ballast, and she went clean over in a gale. The women and the children were all in the hold, and Marion wouldn't leave the children, but Munokoa managed to get out through the hatch, and she and a couple of other Palmerston people swam around till next day, when they sighted Aitutaki. Although there was a tremendous sea running they managed to swim to the island. When they tried to land one of the men got smashed on the reef, but Munokoa and the other chap got ashore. That morning on Palmerston old William came out of his house and said to the people, "Marion is dead," he said. "She 's drowned," he said. "I 've seen her combing out her wet hair." And it wasn't till two months later that they heard what had happened.'

On 31st March 1926 one of the worst hurricanes struck the island. In the early morning there hadn't been a breath of wind, but the weather was oppressive. William Marsters II, who was now the patriarch, kept looking at his barometer. 'You could see the hand jiggling about. "There 's something around," he said. "There 's something around, and we 're going to get it."' He gave orders that every one should go to 'the mountain,' a small hillock about eighteen feet above sea level, the highest point of the island. He had hardly done so when the storm broke. The sea rushed over everything. Many people who had gone to their houses to save a few belongings were caught. One woman was drowned. If others had not been strong swimmers they would have been carried away. Lumps of sharp coral and big stones which were being hurtled about in the water added to the danger. Those who could get to the high ground climbed into trees and were compelled to stay there until the storm abated, twelve hours later. Every pig and chicken on the island was lost: plantations were destroyed. The only house that survived was the one built by 'the old man.' In spite of subsequent hurricanes, including one in 1935 when two of the eight islets were washed away completely, the house is standing to-day.

CHAPTER FIFTEEN

S IMI HAD BEEN URGING ME to visit 'the volcanic,' meaning the crater that was left by the eruption at Matavanu in 1905, and, weakly, I had allowed myself once again to be persuaded by him. Although other authorities had disagreed, he had insisted that the journey was an easy one and that I would find 'plenty-make-picture' at the summit. He could borrow a horse which would carry me most of the way, he said, and Ata, a friend of his who knew every foot of the track, would come with us as guide.

So on horseback, with my two companions on foot, I set out one morning at dawn. The air was still and sweet, with a faint tang of wood smoke; no breath of wind stirred the fronds, wet leaves were spangled with cobwebs, crisp ferns gave out a pungent fragrance. After heavy rain the earth, replete with moisture, awaited the heat of the day. For the first few miles it was easy going, and the horse seemed familiar with the track; if it made a sudden divergence it was only because it knew of slippery rocks that lay ahead.

Simi had said that the crater to which we were going was 'dead.' But Simi's English was not scientifically accurate. I remembered the great amphitheatre at Solfatara in the Bay of Naples, acres of crusted soil with steam spitting through crevices and a lake of boiling lava near its centre. At one time *it* had been thought to be dead. Perhaps I would see something of that kind. I remembered Mont Pelée, in Martinique, which twenty-seven years after its eruption was still giving off fumes and pouring out streams of water too hot for human touch. St. Pierre at its foot had been a flourishing town until, on Ascension Day 1902, that incandescent avalanche had plunged down the mountain side, smothering and blasting all in its way. Perhaps Simi's 'dead volcanic' might show signs of life.

I thought of the crater lake at Waimangu in New Zealand, whose ethereal beauty almost hides its sinister significance. Deep in the great cleft lies this lake of clear blue boiling water, veiled by floating wisps of its own steam, like the frozen waters of a fiord from whose surface the powdered snow is blown. And not far from Waimangu is the Geyser Valley at Wairakei. Fear-inspiring, spiritually exalting. On all sides sulphurous fumes belching from gaping scars, fantastic forms surrounding each geyser pool. Here plumes of water shoot high into the air to fall cascading over saffron-tinted terraces, crinkled and curled as a fleece from Astrakhan; there around a pool crouch petrified beasts in strange contortions, their scabrous hides pearl-grey and lilac, rose-pink and gold. Even as one watches, the ground beneath one's feet vibrates, and the water in a pool seethes and hurls itself high into the air, to descend in a smother of foam into the boiling stream below. On all sides weird rhythmic gurglings, on all sides quivering pools, turquoise, viridian and jade, rust and rose-red, coloured by the minerals at their source. Interspersed among them are pools of boiling mud, some white, some pink, some grey, spitting and spluttering. Strange to relate, the growth of plant life in the valley is luxuriant; trees, ferns, and mosses seem unaffected by the seeping exhalations, even tender grasses lean over and trail in the scalding streams.

Recollections came to an end when the track petered out in the bush, and it became impossible to go further on horseback. Tying the horse to a tree, we continued on foot. Trailing vines now tripped our feet, hanging vines noosed our necks; fallen branches obstructed our progress, fallen trees hidden in the undergrowth barked our shins. We fought our way through this jungle for an hour—to find ourselves under the tree beside the horse.

'I think we lose track,' said Simi.

'I'm sure we did,' I said.

Simi, with the air of a commanding officer, now ordered Ata to go and find the way, saying that he and I would stay where we were and await his return. Ata disappeared into the bush, and Simi and I sat down. At first the mosquitoes came a few at a time, soon they came in clouds. Simi was talkative; I was not.

'What about copra?' he asked.

'What about it?' I replied.

'What about price?'

'I don't know anything about it.'

'You friend of Queen Victoria?'

'No.'

'What you think about vanilla?'

'I don't think about it.'

Then he began to tell me about Samoa. Samoa, he said, is the country where men are born loving each other. I made no comment on that. He said that his wife wanted me to make a drawing of their baby. 'I say to my wife, "Kipingi best drawer in world; good as photo."' My reply was not encouraging.

At last we heard our guide calling, and we rose up in eagerness. But as we went along the sound seemed to come from a variety of directions, and it became more and more difficult to follow. After half an hour we discovered that we were chasing an echo. When after another half-hour we got back to the horse we found Ata asleep under the tree.

Once again we plunged among the vines and creepers, with the added distraction, this time, of an undergrowth just thick enough to hide the sharp lava boulders through which it pushed its way. It wasn't till the sun was at its zenith and the heat of the day at its worst that we emerged on to the open lava field and saw the crater ahead—two miles of climbing before us.

The lava over which we now had to travel presented a tortured surface, metallic in appearance, crumpled, corrugated, jagged. For the most part it retained its molten forms, smooth and glistening, but in places it was rough and broken like cinders. Here and there it was twisted and coiled upon itself as though it were rope. Where trees had stood there were hollows, the moulds of the burnt-out trunks. Where steam had once formed under thin layers of the lava there were blisters and tumours. The eruption had continued for several years and layer after layer had been superimposed, sometimes in a thin crust, sometimes in a mass of clinker-like scoria.

It was irksome walking. Every step had to be watched. There were cavities covered by the thinnest veneer, at any moment a shin might be cut; there were wide areas covered with rough brittle lumps, at any moment an ankle might be twisted. The heat of the sun reflected from the lava was almost as intense as the direct rays from above.

Before the eruption there had been a deep and tortuous valley where we were walking. Now the level was above that of the surrounding countryside, and the lava was a thousand feet deep below us. And, as the valley had filled, the viscid flood had spread out fan-wise, moving slowly, inexorably—perhaps a few yards in the hour, rarely faster than a man can walk—searing, cremating, and destroying without purpose everything in its course, until amid clouds of steam and with volleys of explosions it poured into the sea.

'Lots of houses under lava,' said Simi. 'Lots of churches, lots of graves, all under lava, damn' funny.'

'Too many men work Sunday that time,' said Ata. 'They work Sunday just like other day—Monday, Friday, Thursday. They say, we work all days this year, we millionaires next year. But God he say, "Pouf! That no good." Then he send fire. But *taupou* not under lava,' he added. 'That show she go straight up in heaven. Very good girl.'

By a curious freak, in all its unrelenting progress the lava had left one small space untouched, unharmed—the grave of a *taupou* in Saleaula village. For some reason, perhaps geological, it had encircled that spot instead of flowing over it. To-day the grave can still be seen, deep in the solid lava, the only opening in that crusted wilderness. When I asked about it, I was told that the girl had died about two years before the eruption. She had been held in great honour by her people, and old folk who knew her said that it was because of her great virtue that the grave was not destroyed.

At last we reached the summit. Simi was right in one respect—'the volcanic' *was* dead. There was nothing to be seen but a large hole whose sides had fallen in, whose sides were indeed still crumbling, so that it was dangerous to approach their edges. There was no lake. Except for a few ferns in the crevices of the lava, and a few small shrubs within the crater, there was no sign of life. And by now it was two o'clock and the sun was blastingly hot. And, contrary to Simi's aesthetic judgment, there was nothing that I could see to draw; if there had been, I shouldn't have wanted to draw it.

So, after a short rest we set out on the homeward journey. We hadn't gone a quarter of a mile before my guides missed the track. We hadn't gone half a mile before we were lost among high ridges of porous, brittle, flint-edged boulders. And the more we searched and the further we retraced our steps the less chance there seemed of our ever escaping from those maze-like mountains of scoria. Climbing cliffs is often easier than descending them; when going up one can see the faces of the precipices ahead, when coming down one often sees them all too suddenly.

Again and again my guides and I got separated, and each time we met it seemed more difficult to extricate ourselves from the labyrinth. Finally in desperation I eluded them deliberately, and struck a course on my own. Three hours later I reached the edge of the bush.

But there was no sign of Simi or Ata. I called and called again, without reply. Had they gone on without me, or were they still finding their way across the lava? If they had gone on I knew that a search party would be sent out, and that at latest I would be found next morning; if they had not reached the bush before me they would see me waiting for them as they came, on the highest level of lava I could find, with my shirt held aloft on a stick.

It was only after a long hour of waiting that they appeared, their legs cut and bleeding. They had not even seen the track the whole way down. But I was in no mood to offer sympathy. It was already getting dusk, and when we got inside the bush it was almost dark. Again and again we lost the way. Backwards and forwards through that jungle we went, tripped and tripped again, almost choked at every step by vines and creepers invisible in the dark. We only found the horse when Ata fell over the rope that tethered it.

Then for me, on horseback, it was impossible to see my guides. I couldn't even see the ground below me. I could only leave it to the horse. And all the time I wondered how long the girth—a single strip of bark— would hold.

Under the dense mango-trees there was inky darkness, but in the palm groves the rising moon cast weird shadows across the path. At times they resembled fallen trees. I remembered a donkey that as a boy I used to drive in Ireland. Every time it came to a shadow on the road it tried to jump it, cart and all. It was an animal that had won many races on the flat and would have made a wonderful steeple-chaser. We reached home at midnight, just as a search party was leaving the village to look for us.

CHAPTER SIXTEEN

THERE IS SOMETHING very charming in the gesture of an elderly lady of comfortable presence who, when sitting almost naked in a pool, invites you to join her in the bath. 'Plenty room, you come alongside here.'

She said it so sweetly that it would have been ungallant to refuse. 'You want soap?' she added, throwing a long yellow bar of it across to me.

'You speak English very well,' I said, as I sat down on a shelving rock in the water.

'Flaherty, he teach me English. You know Flaherty? He come to this village, Safune, make movie. One day he say to me: "Losa, what you think, you like me put you in picture? Then every one in world see you." You see me in picture?' she asked.

'In *Moana of the South Seas*, the girl making tapa?' I suggested, chancing a long shot.

'Yes, that's me!' she said, delighted. 'You see me? That's what Flaherty say—every one in world see me.'

A girl of about sixteen came along, sat in the pool, and began to wash her hair with a lemon.

'That my daughter,' said Losa, pointing to the girl. 'She like me when Flaherty make photo. Her name Sina.'

'Is she afraid of eels?' I asked.

'What! You know story about pool? About Sina and eel, long time ago?'

'Yes,' I said, 'I know about Sina, and Bob Flaherty is an old friend of mine.'

The story of Sina to which Losa referred is one that occurs again and again in varying forms throughout Polynesia. A girl of that name, when walking across marshy ground, found a small eel. She took it home and kept it alive in a wooden bowl filled with water, feeding it every day just as Hina in Tonga used to feed her pet shark. By and by, when the eel grew too big for the bowl, she carried it to a small pool near her home and again, later, when her pet grew too big for that, she transferred it to a larger pool —the very one, according to Samoan tradition, in which I was then sitting. The water there is cool and sparkling, bubbling up from a spring in the coral and flowing into the brackish lagoon that separates the village of Safune from the mainland. It is a favourite bathing place, and at most times of the day women will be seen scrubbing and pounding clothes either in the stream that leads from it to the lagoon or, near by, in the lagoon itself.

One day when Sina had carried her daily basket of food to the eel she climbed into a frangipane-tree that overhung the pool to pick some blossoms for a garland, but in doing so she happened to shake the tree so that the blossoms fell into the water. When she went into the water to gather the flowers the eel came to her and, twining himself about her body, embraced her more intimately than decorously. Horrified, Sina fled from the pool. She left her home, she left her village. Fearful of telling any one, she ran along the coast until she reached the village of Safotu. There she halted awhile on the shore, only to see the eel watching her from behind a boulder on the reef. Then from day to day, from place to place, the creature pursued her. She could not escape it. It haunted her. The weeks went by and the months, and always, at unexpected moments, she would see the hated features staring at her. Even when she married and crossed over to Upolu, the eel followed her. One day when working in her taro plantation she saw its eyes peering from the swamp. This time she screamed, and when in answer to her cries her husband reached her, she told him what had happened. Then the eel spoke to her. 'I know that you are going to kill me,' it said, 'but, before you do so, let me speak. I am not an eel; I am a high chief of Fiji who, hearing of your beauty, put an enchantment upon myself that I might reach you. And now you hate me. This one thing I ask, that when I am dead you cut off my head and bury it in the ground. Then there will grow a tree that will bear you food and drink. It will give you posts for your houses and leaves to make thatch for your houses; its leaves, too, will make baskets for you and torches, and its roots and the juice of its bark will be medicine for you when you are sick. It will give you everything that you need. And when you hold the fruit in your hand you will see my face, always.'

Losa, who was still beside me, picked up an empty coco-nut shell that lay near. 'You see face of eel?' she said, pointing to the three depressions at one end. 'Those two his eyes, that one his mouth; that's where tree grows—out of his mouth. That's how first coco-nut came to Samoa.'

In this story the symbolism of the serpent and the tree of life will be recognized. Throughout all mythologies it is recurrent. All over the world, too, one will find a similar dread of the eel or serpent. In Southern Italy the idea that snakes make love to women is prevalent. In India and Japan it is believed that girls are in danger of being assaulted by serpents, and the same holds true of Abyssinia, Algeria, Malabar, and many other countries.

The name Sina, like Hina in Tonga, is common in Samoa, not only for those maidens whose feet are firmly planted on the ground, but for those mythical semi-mortals who in leading roles make their appearance on the stage of legend. There was one of their number who married a king of Fiji, and is said to have brought several kinds of fish from Fiji to Samoa; but she, I think, has been confused with Sina, the moon goddess—*masina*, the moon—who in her various phases brings the spawning creatures towards the shore. There was another Sina who was married to Tangaloa-langi, the supreme god of the heavens. Her parents, who were crippled, lived at Neiafu, at the western end of Savai'i, but because of their infirmity they were unable to gather the breadfruit from their trees. Their daughter, therefore, sent the east and the north-east winds to go and blow down the fruit; but Neiafu is sheltered from the east and the north, and the winds were not strong enough. Therefore she ordered the west wind, which comes unimpeded over a thousand miles of ocean, to do the work. This west wind did the job all too thoroughly, for it blew down not only sufficient for immediate needs but far more than they could hope to use. It happened, however, that near by there was a hole in the rocks, some two feet deep and about as wide—you can see it to-day —and into this the old folk threw what they could not consume. Some months later they found the fruit fermented and attractive. They kneaded it into cakes, and they cooked it in their *umu*, and they ate it with relish; and that is how *masi*, one of the staple foods of Samoa, became known.

There was another Sina who was carried across the sea by a shark. At that time all sharks were known as *mango*, but, after Sina had alighted safely on shore and said 'Thank you' politely, the shark has been known as *malie*— 'to thank,' in Samoan. And yet another, less fortunate, girl used to bathe in a pool, and 'one day crab who live in pool come along and he want to have Sina for wife. But Sina laugh at crab. So crab catch her and eat her up. Ever since that time you see picture of Sina on that crab's back,' and this I have often seen on the shell of a particular crab that frequents the mouths of streams.

I came across many Sinas in Samoa, but the memory of one in particular remains in my mind. It was when I was staying with an artist called Harding that I met her. Harding belonged to the 'follow nature' school. The more you could imitate nature the greater, he thought, was your art. I had often tried to point out to him my belief that human beings with a few opaque pigments and a few square yards of canvas were little match for the Almighty with the whole range of the spectrum and the whole horizon at His disposal. But Harding could not agree. He had got the slogan 'Follow nature' firmly into his brain and into his work, and both brain and work had suffered accordingly. One evening, after a late meal, we sat in his house going backwards and forwards over the same old argument. Is art a selection of harmonies, or, as Whistler put it, is it just sitting on the piano? Harding's native wife came into the room, and with her another girl, neatly dressed in white, Sina by name. Both sat down and for a while they watched us, without speaking. Harding was theorizing as to whether the retina of each of us creates a similar image, or whether in some cases it might not act as a distorting mirror, when suddenly Sina, looking in my direction, asked: 'When you going to bed?'

'Soon,' I said, for I was tired and only too ready to drop a hint to my host. But Harding paid no attention to the interruption. He went on talking. He wanted to know what the Cubists, the Post-impressionists, and the Surrealists were after, with the inevitable question: 'Did they see things as they painted them?'

Sina interrupted again. 'You married?' she asked.

'Yes,' I answered.

She put her hand to her face and giggled. 'Where your wife?'

'In England.'

'England far away,' she said, with a long-drawn emphasis on the 'far.'

'But I can't see the need of abstraction,' said Harding, recalling my thoughts more appositely than he knew. 'Isn't nature good enough?'

'It certainly is pretty wonderful at times,' I said, 'but I'm not sure at this precise moment whether it is always wise to follow it.'

'I think you're tired,' said Harding.

We climbed out of our long cane chairs, and I said good night to the two girls. Sina seemed a little surprised, a little puzzled; but when I saw her next day she smiled at me as she went by. Bless her little heart.

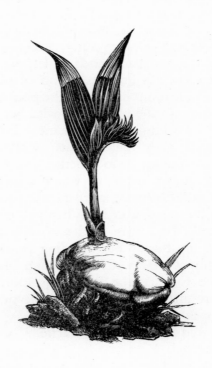

CHAPTER SEVENTEEN

I MISSED SEEING the tidal wave by an hour, the same wave that on 1st April 1946 caused such destruction in the Hawaiian Islands, in the Marquesas, and elsewhere in the Pacific. In Hawaii the death-roll was over a hundred and fifty and there were as many injured. Close on five hundred houses were destroyed and twice that number damaged. At Pitcairn Island marks showed where the waves had struck the cliffs sixty feet above normal; half the fleet of fishing canoes were carried away. In the Marquesas, waves twenty feet high swept inland. The captain of a French schooner who was in those islands at the time wrote: 'I witnessed a terrifying scene of destruction wrought by an onslaught of the sea. No house, no store, no drying-shed remained; trees and coco-nut palms were broken down, and floated at the mercy of the tide.'

The wave was caused by a movement of the sea floor in the deep water south of the Aleutian Islands, over two thousand miles to the north of Hawaii, and it is estimated that it travelled at an average speed of about five hundred miles an hour. But whereas the length of the wave was calculated to be a hundred and twenty-two miles from crest to crest, its height from trough to crest was only two feet, so that at sea it was imperceptible to ships. It was only when it reached the shallow waters near the islands that the retarding influence of the sea floor on the base of the wave caused it to pile on itself and sweep forward like a tidal bore.

On the north coast of Upolu, as at Rarotonga in the Cook Islands, there was nothing more than a spectacular ebb and flow of the water in the harbour. At one moment the sea was high above its normal level, a few moments later the harbour at Apia was drained of water, with vessels of all kinds lying on their sides on the bare coral.

Women and children hurried on to the naked reef to gather the shell-fish now miraculously exposed, and as quickly scrambled to shore again, scarce able to escape the inrush of the tide. People began to run about the streets of the town; sober tradesmen became melodramatic at the thought of losing their merchandise. The governor was sent for, but he was as powerless as Canute to alter marine events.

A European, far out in the bay, intent on adjusting the engine of his launch, suddenly found the propeller immovable and a heavy list to starboard. A moment later, with the engine stopped, his vessel was travelling faster than it had ever done before, and he got on deck barely in time to fend it from the pier. Five minutes later it was again high and dry.

On the south side of Upolu there was no evidence of anything untoward taking place. In answer to an invitation from my friend Tame Ah Kuoi, I had driven over the new cross-island road that morning. There had been thunder and lightning, and rain that seemed a match for the deluge of leaves that curtained either side of the road, hanging in festoons from vines and creepers, smothering the tall trees. But on the south side of the island the general level of the sea had remained unchanged, and I knew nothing of what had happened at Apia until after my return to the capital a week later. Tame, who keeps a trading store in the village of Savaia, gave me a hearty welcome. A *fale* had been decorated. Chiefs brought kava roots and presents of tapa cloth. There were rather more chiefs than might have been expected because men from the district were going shark fishing that night, and when such an expedition is planned the chiefs like to gather together to 'pray' for success. 'It is like a pastor asking the congregation to pray for someone who is ill,' I was told. 'They direct their thoughts towards that sick person, and that gives him strength.' Here in Samoa there is the same ritual connected with shark fishing that I had found in Tonga.

So that evening at Savaia we sat quietly in the *fale*, and I told them fairy-tales from Ireland, and they told me of strange happenings in their own islands; and every now and again there would be a pause in the conversation while we thought of the shark fishers. Then the threads of romance would be gathered together again, and we would continue with our stories.

It was the first time for several months that one of the party had been present at a gathering. He had been ill, and unable to walk. He told us that he had felt as if there were a great weight on his legs; he could only be comfortable when lying down. The native medical practitioner had visited him again and again and had tried many treatments, but none of them had had any effect: he could not even guess at the cause of the trouble. Eventually, however, the N.M.P. said it might be some kind of Samoan sickness, and he suggested that they should consult a 'wise man.' So the chief sent his son to a man whom he knew, and he told him all the symptoms. Then this expert gave the boy some liquid in a bamboo stem, saying that it was to be rubbed on the sick man's legs. 'And tell your father,' he said, 'that from now until he stands upright as the centre post of a house, and until he walks again as freely as a heron on the reef, I will eat no food.'

The chief's son reached home next day. No sooner was the medicine applied than all pain left the sick man's limbs. At that very moment, too, the chief heard the voices of two spirits saying to him: 'You bad old man, you wicked old man.' Then he could hear them running from the house and breaking down all the plants outside, and as their voices died away in the distance they were still calling abuse at him. It was they who had caused the trouble; they had been sitting on his legs. And then, though he had been unable to walk for six months, he found that he could move about freely and that he was completely cured.

When we asked him if he could account in any way for the presence of the spirits, he said that he thought they might be two women with whom he used to enjoy himself as a young man. They had died recently, and he thought that perhaps they had come back to be with him and to prevent him enjoying himself with other women who were still alive.

Then we were told of a spirit named To'uto'u, who frequents the neighbouring village of Mulivai. He appears as a young man, about six feet tall, wearing a white *lavalava*. Every one can see him, though no one can touch him. He is friendly to the village and shows many kindnesses to the people. For instance, if a party of visitors is on its way, he will appear on the *malae* carrying two baskets on a shoulder pole, to show that extra food will soon be needed. And should any people from another village attempt any harm in the Mulivai plantations, he will appear in various guises and frighten them away. But To'uto'u is very puritanical, and upholds the rule of the village that no one may bathe naked in the stream. Once there was a woman who jumped into the water without her *lavalava*, and during the night, while she slept in her *fale*, To'uto'u came along and took her away and hanged her on the top of a tall tree, and it was a tree so tall that no one could climb it.

All the time as we listened to the stories the chiefs were rolling sennit. It is held to be a worthy occupation for men of rank, on all but the most ceremonious occasions. Each one sits with a bundle of coco-nut fibre before him, selecting a few of the fibres at a time and rolling them between palm and thigh into short strands. When sufficient of these strands have been accumulated, he will plait them into a single braid.

'In your country,' said a chief to me, 'only a few men can make nails, but in Samoa every one can make nails.' As he said this he pointed to the sennit beside him; then, with a smile, he added: 'Samoan nails need no hammer.' It is not surprising that sennit-making is such a constant occupation, for the joints of even a small house require many miles of the cord.

Stories continued late into the evening, only interrupted by occasional remarks about the weather. It was raining hard. The wind had risen. It would be very rough where the men were fishing. They would be away until the following evening. My contentment grew that I had not joined the expedition. Yet, late the following after-noon when the fishermen returned with eight sharks, I was sorry that I had not been with them. They showed me the sennit noose they had used—five years old and as good as new. They said it would last another five years if cared for.

CHAPTER EIGHTEEN

'FAR OUT in the whole world each nation is noted or famous for a thing. For instance, Great Britain and her fleet, the United States of America and her riches, and the other different parts of the world of which I cannot have enough time to explain. For what is Manono famous? Manono is famous for her fleet. The biggest and most famous fleet in the world was in Britain, but the biggest and most famous fleet in Samoa was in Manono. Manono was proud of their fleet. Their fleet was more than thirty boats of different kinds. The chief reason of building this fleet was to fight against other villages and to carry their famous king, Tamafainga, anywhere he want.'

From the above essay of a Samoan student one rightly gathers that this small island of Manono, lying midway between Upolu and Savai'i, was at one time locally famous as a maritime power. And not only was it famous for its fleet, but for the willingness of its people to join in a fight. It is said that when a new king was elected on the main island of Upolu, Manono, instead of the more usual presents of food and fine mats, sent a gift of clubs and spears, as a symbol of its desire to assist in any war upon which the new king might embark.

There was no suggestion of anything but a perpetual peace on the day that I crossed the two miles of lagoon that divides Manono from Upolu. The sea was calm. Six oarsmen sang as they rowed. Tame had come with me as interpreter, and Lepale, a chief from the village of Savaia, as my orator.

We were received by a crowd of men, women, and children who led us from the shore to the guest-house. It was a very famous *fale*, I was told. 'Anywhere all round the whole of Savai'i and Upolu, if any one is in trouble he can run to this *fale*, and when he gets inside no one can touch him.' It is the seventh house to be built on the site, and there are three pieces of wood in its construction which have been part of every earlier building. 'If one house blown down or go rotten, those three pieces of wood put away, made safe, till chief say we build new house.'

The speeches at the kava ceremony which followed my arrival were even more complimentary than usual. This time I was likened to Nafanua, the war goddess. She had left great power to the village, and I, by my writing, would also confer great power.

That night there was a rehearsal of a play which the islanders were going to perform in Apia, to raise money for the repair of their church, and I was invited to attend. The long *fale* was lit by a single oil lamp. Its sides, lined with spectators, and its rafters and roof, were lost in shadows. In the centre a few mats had been laid on the coral floor, and towards one end a small table and two stools. This was the stage and its properties, and here the many characters came and went, covering imaginary distances by walking up and down the mats. Here they danced, sang, acted, and played the fool in a combination of ballet, opera, and play. A shrill blast of a whistle, followed by a flourish of guitars, was sufficient to mark a change of scene. There were many actors, all male, and each in the course of the evening played many parts. The action was brisk, and the story wove its unpredictable way through a long sequence of scenes in which policemen and doctors, anxious parents and lovely maidens, Chinese vendors and Indian messenger boys, an American millionaire and a fierce and irrepressible pantomime dog, came and went in bewildering succession, to the accompaniment of a running commentary and frequent interpolations from the master of ceremonies, who was seated at the side of the stage.

A few weeks later in the capital I was to see the full flowering of this entertainment. By then those items that would be the most remunerative had been developed to the full. Scenes had been devised to touch not only the spectator's heart but also his pocket. A woman with a child in her arms is travelling in a bus—represented by eight men on their knees on the floor. When the conductor attempts to collect her fare, she has no money. She is thereupon arrested, her child is taken from her, and amid great lamentation she is hauled off to the prison. Will not the audience help to pay this poor woman's fare? A shower of silver is thrown on to the stage.

In another scene a man commits a murder. It is entirely accidental and he is in no way to blame; nevertheless he is taken to court and convicted. Either he must pay a heavy fine or be hanged. He sings a heart-wringing song before being led to the scaffold. This time a veritable torrent of coins saves the unfortunate man's life. They raised £70 that night in Apia. All was acted with the verve of a harlequinade, neither was there any lack of slap-stick buffoonery; the baby was thrown about the stage, the murderer was bitten in his bottom by the dog. There is little pictorial art in Samoa, but they have a fine sense of the drama. Indeed, on one occasion, a stage wedding in the European style was taken so seriously by the leading actors that they set up house together afterwards without further rites of church. But it was during the rehearsal at Manono and at other times on less public occasions, in the villages, that I saw the greatest fun. Scenes that were possible in domestic privacy were not suitable for public performance under clerical patronage. A courting scene in which the girl's mother constantly changed places with her daughter to the discomfiture of the suitor was only surpassed when, in the natural denouement, the old lady was again found where her daughter was expected.

Between that rehearsal on Manono and the finished performance in Apia important events occurred for me. Two days after the rehearsal, days in which I had done little beyond wander about the island and make an occasional drawing, I noticed that all the chiefs were in solemn conclave. They were sitting in the house of Leiataua, the high chief, and it was obvious that they were deliberating on some matter of serious import. Each time that I passed that *fale* I noticed that they looked at me as if I were the subject of their discussion. I began to feel uncomfortable. Had I in any way offended them? Had I inadvertently committed some serious breach of etiquette? People in the village, too, seemed to be keeping more at a distance, a sort of respectful distance. What had I done? At midday I broached the subject to Tame.

'I think they are going to give you a title,' he said.

He had hardly spoken when an orator came to say that I was wanted in Leiataua's house. There I found his family assembled, all but Leiataua himself. But I was told nothing of what was to happen. Three old women took charge of me. They stripped me to the minimum, and rubbed oil into my skin—my arms and chest glistened with it. They brought yards of ornate tapa cloth and wound it about my middle, securing it with a sash of the same material. They hung an *ula* of flowers about my neck, and put a hibiscus blossom behind my right ear. Bracelets of shining leaves were tied around my wrists. I was turned and twisted, and patted on the back and chest.

When at length they were satisfied with my appearance, I was conducted back to my own *fale*. Here all the chiefs of the island had assembled, and, in addition, several visiting chiefs, twenty-three in all. I was shown to my appointed place, and sat down cross-legged. The *fale* was full; every one of the encircling posts was occupied, and some of the lesser chiefs were seated between posts. Then Leiataua, through his orator, announced that they had decided to confer on me a title. Henceforth I was to be of the 'royal family.' Whether I stayed in Samoa or whether I went away, it would always be the same; the village was my village, and they were my brothers.

Then each chief threw a kava root on to a mat provided for the purpose, and the mat was laid before me. In the distance I could hear the beating of drums and blowing of conch shells, and soon a band of warriors appeared, decorated with leaves and flowers and singing a song of triumph. They carried before them a large shrub of kava, freshly dug, the soil still clinging to its roots. 'Green kava,' whispered Tame, 'only for the highest chiefs.' The young men placed the bush in front of the *fale*, then, marching round, took their places behind the chiefs.

Now the customary discussion arose as to which of the orators should have the honour of making the speech. Each one put forward his claim. The argument was protracted more than usual. Finally the honour was adjudged to a young man who had but recently become an orator, but who held a senior title. The speech began. Tame translated it to me.

'On behalf of Leiataua, I, Futi, am selected by Manono to make ceremony for the election of you, Tusitala, as one of our chiefs. Kava has been presented to Lepale, your orator, for you and for the kava bowl. At the time when the kava is ready we will drink—a cup to you, whom we now name Tamafainga, a cup to Leiataua, a cup to Tame who translates, a cup to Lepale, your orator, and many cups for the chiefs of Manono and the other islands. And this very precious day we lift our hearts to God to protect you, Tamafainga, for the beginning of your title. Other white men when they come to Samoa have sometimes been given titles, but no white man or Samoan ever before had this title, only the first Tamafainga. You are the second to be called by it. That will be your name through all Samoa. You are now a chief of this village. Whatever you do anywhere in Samoa, we will always help you. This title will be with you till the end of the world.'

While I was being thus addressed, the *taupou* and her assistants were preparing kava. When it was served, I was given the first cup, Leiataua receiving the final one.

More speeches followed, most of them addressed to me, some spoken on my behalf by Lepale. Then came the presentation of a roast pig, a coco-nut, and a piece of tapa cloth. When these symbols of food and raiment had been laid before me, Lepale, standing outside the *fale*, in a loud voice announced to the village that the presentation had taken place. Then he made it known that I had given sundry cases of Fiji biscuits and tins of *pisupo*. As he finished speaking, I could hear in the distance the voices of orators proclaiming my new name through the village.

That ended formalities. Now that official proceedings were at an end we would drink kava as becoming to those of one family. This time as a high chief in his own village, I, Tamafainga, was given the final cup.

The ceremony being over the visitors retired, but Leiataua and the other chiefs of Manono remained in the *fale*. They wanted to tell me of the first Tamafainga. He was a direct descendant of Nafanua, the goddess of war, they said, and it was for that reason that he had been powerful enough to unite the warring peoples of Samoa and bring them under one king. Because of my writings they believed that I was going to unite all the people of the world, and that was why they had chosen to give me that title. They wanted to tell me that the first Tamafainga had been one of their greatest men. It was he who had brought so much renown to Manono that the island was still honoured as one of the most important districts of Samoa. It was known as 'The Family in the Sea.' I must always remember that I belonged to that family. Though our parents were different, we were now brothers.

Leiataua then produced some heirlooms of which the most important were a fish-hook and a piece of turtle shell. Many of the chiefs present had not seen these before, and passed them from hand to hand, greatly interested. The hook is made of whale-bone, pearl shell, and turtle shell. It is of divine origin, having been given by the Sun to his son, when he married a princess of Fiji. It was given in lieu of the pigs, canoes, and weapons which are the customary contribution of a bridegroom's family at a wedding. Many crises and accidents have overtaken the hook since then, but it is now safe in the custody of Leiataua. The fragment of turtle shell was brought from Upolu by the conquering armies of Manono many long

years ago.   To-day on special occasions the *taupou* wears
it round her neck as a decoration.

'Do not forget,' said Leiataua, when he rose to leave me,
'you are now a chief of Manono.   When you wish for
anything you must not ask for it, you must command and
it will be done.'   That night I realized that my wishes
were commands, even in retrospect.   I had inquired if
nowadays they always wore European dress when dancing.
At a *fiafia* given in my honour, Leiataua's own daughter
To'oa, the *taupou* of the village, danced in the dress of
olden times.

CHAPTER NINETEEN

WHEN I GOT TO APIA a few days later I was still feeling somewhat elated at my new dignity. As I arrived at Tina's, Frank appeared with a bag of golf clubs over his shoulder.

'Hallo, Robert. How's things?'

'Pretty good,' I replied. 'They made me a chief.'

'Just a moment,' he said, taking down the telephone receiver. There was a pause while he waited for the number. 'Hallo! Is that you, Nance? Yes, it's me. I did it in ninety-nine! Yes, the whole round. Went all out—beat them flat.'

I left him to it. Tina was counting shrimps as I passed the kitchen. 'Come in, come in! Did you have a good time?'

'Yes,' I said. 'They made me a chief.'

'D' you know, those damn' people at Peak Mason's only sent me three dozen shrimps and I ordered four,' she said.

I recalled the remark of my eldest son, aged six at the time, when I announced to him that his mother had borne twins. 'Look at my new engine,' he said.

I did not mention my own new toy again for a few days. Then, thinking to learn a little more about my namesake, I dropped in on a friend, Jack Ellis, whose library had already been of much service to me.

'Tamafainga!' he exclaimed. 'The worst cannibal Samoa has ever known—he's notorious!'

'But,' I said, 'the man only died in 1830, and it's well known that there has been no cannibalism in Samoa for several hundred years.'

Ellis went to his shelves and picked out Williams's

127

Missionary Enterprises. He read: 'The people of Upolu, wearied with the outrages and oppressions of this tyrannical monster, whose rapacious grasp neither wives, daughters, nor property escaped, who had power of life and death, and who was actually worshipped as a god, had waylaid and murdered him.'

'Sounds to me a bit prejudiced,' I said.

'The man wouldn't have been in his job if he wasn't prejudiced,' said Ellis. 'No good those early missionaries being broad-minded. They had to be fanatical or they wouldn't have got anywhere. Let's see another authority.'

He took down a more recent publication, Kramer's *Samoan Islands*, and quoted: 'The cruel and bloodthirsty Tamafainga, from whom no woman or girl was safe——'

'Hearsay,' I said.

'May I ask what you're talking about?' said Father Carrol, coming in at the open door.

'You're the very man I want, Father,' I said. 'I've just been given the title of a great hero, and this fellow, with his books, is trying to blacken the reputation of my namesake.'

'If it's Tamafainga you're speaking of,' said Father Carrol, 'and I think I heard the name, it might be not unfair to say that he exceeded his privileges.'

'But don't all men of spirit exceed their privileges, now and again?' I asked.

Father Carrol smiled and paused a moment. 'Maybe you're right,' he said.

'He had ninety-nine wives,' said Ellis, 'and you can see a building on Manono with that number of stones, and a space left for the hundredth, which was never filled because the old villain was murdered before he made his century.'

'And that's not true, either,' I said. 'I've made a drawing of those stones, and I was told the story on Manono, and it doesn't apply to Tamafainga at all but to another chief, by name Vaovasa. Anyway,' I said, 'what's a hundred wives to a chief in those days? On the island of Tofua in Tonga there's a place known as "A hundred to

Tungi." It's where a king found his hundredth bride. And that's a poor effort compared with Solomon.'

'Autres temps, autres mœurs,' said Father Carrol.

'Indeed,' I said, 'it isn't only *autres temps* either, for the present king of Saudi Arabia has been married more than a hundred and fifty times.'

'You'll find all about your hero's death in this,' said Ellis, handing me a manuscript by the late Brother Fred Henry of the Marist Mission. 'Take it home with you, if you like, and study it.'

I took it home, and this is what I found:

'When the news of his murder reached Manono it produced the greatest consternation. Their fleet was immediately dispatched to fetch the remains of their lord and high chief. Reaching Faleasi'u and seeing the mutilated body of Tamafainga, the party manifested their sorrow and grief by tearing out their hair and beating their heads and breasts with sharp stones till the blood flowed. Then they placed the body of the king and his slain companions with the greatest reverence in a war canoe, and sailed away in profound silence. Manono was soon reached, and when the people perceived that their renowned high priest had been desecrated in such a horrible fashion, their lamentations changed into frenzied cries for revenge.' The same author goes on to say that as soon as Manono had determined on a war of revenge against the people of A'ana who had committed the murder, she was joined by 'nearly the whole of Samoa—yea, even Atua, the old ally of A'ana.' That doesn't suggest universal rejoicing at his death, I thought.

The Russian navigator Kotzebue, who called at Manono in 1824, met Tamafainga and spoke to him, and records that 'his face was engaging, revealing intellect and reflection, his behaviour modest and decorous.' Of course Tamafainga was 'bloodthirsty.' It was nothing uncommon in those days. Of course he liked women. 'Twould be a queer world if men didn't. What's more, all women love a hero; his opportunities must have been prodigious.

I don't doubt that a great deal of what was said against the man was true, but I incline to the idea that much of it was exaggerated for the benefit of the listeners. Polynesians have a polite way of saying what they think you would like to hear. On one occasion in Samoa, I heard a girl telling an ethnologist, in answer to his inquiries, a most distressing story of how at the age of sixteen she had been waylaid in the dark. Her eyes brimmed with tears as she gave the most circumstantial details. Her assailant was still in prison, she said, serving a long sentence. I was unable to understand her words, but from the way she hung her head, and at times was too overcome with emotion to continue speaking, I realized the import of her story. Later in the day, when the ethnologist confronted her with the fact that it was a complete fabrication, she threw back her head and laughed with the greatest delight. 'So you found me out!' was her only comment.

Another instance of natives willing to oblige, while indulging their own sense of humour, is to be found in Labillardière's *Vocabulary of the Friendly Isles*, which he compiled while on his journey in search of La Pérouse. At Tonga, when questioning the people about their numerical terms, all went well while they discussed the tens and hundreds and even the thousands, but when he asked them for words not only for a million but for ten million, a hundred million, a thousand million, and others up to a thousand million million, they very rightly considered that the occasion was one deserving levity, and they gave him a series of highly obscene words which he subsequently published in his vocabulary, having no idea of their real meaning.

While on Manono I had also made a drawing of one of the few natural sources of fresh water on the island, a cluster of small pools set deep among stones. At one

time there was a river on Manono, but no fresh water on the neighbouring island of Apolima; and there was a spirit living on Apolima who was very jealous of Manono for that reason, so much so that he would often come across the narrow strait between the two islands and try to steal the stream. It was necessary for the Manono people always to have one or two people watching, lest their river be stolen. But one day the spirit came over and, having managed to elude the watchers, knelt down and not only quenched his thirst but drank up the whole stream, leaving the river bed entirely dry. The guardians of the water saw what had happened only when it was too late; but no sooner had they realized the tragedy than they gave chase. They hunted that spirit all around the island, and three times they caught him, though each time he managed to get away. However, while they had a hold on him they tickled him, and when they tickled him he could not help laughing, and each time that he laughed he could not help spluttering up a little of the water out of his mouth, and

that is what made the springs in the three villages of
Manono. In the end the spirit managed to return to
Apolima, and there he spat out all the water that was left
in his stomach, and that was how Apolima got its only
stream.

Apolima, the crown of a submerged volcano, is a
charming little island. On one side, through a narrow
pass, the sea enters the crater and forms a harbour around
which the only village on the island has been built. The
stream that once belonged to Manono is there for all to see.

CHAPTER TWENTY

TINA SAW TO IT that I had all the models I needed, whether it was her handmaid Tailua, who put aside her cooking while I drew; or Lita who when dancing showed not the slightest trace of self-consciousness, but when asked to hold any pose for even a moment dissolved into a giggling tangle; or old Manita who sat immobile as a bronze. Tailua would sit as in a dream, a large hibiscus behind one ear, her dark hair cascading over the white flowers about her neck. When Lita danced, not only every finger but every joint of every finger played its part. In Europe the emphasis in most dancing is on the legs, in the Cook Islands and Tahiti it is on the hips, but in Samoa it is on the arms and hands. Manita's face gave no hint of what was in her mind as she sat on the balcony looking across the lagoon; for all that I could tell it might have been a grandchild on the reef, a lost pig in the bush, or the latest 'comic' at the cinema that occupied her thoughts.

Many a time just then I, too, would sit on my balcony looking across the lagoon, for I was soon to leave Samoa. In the early morning sea and sky shone with nacreous light.   Tall clouds, motionless on the horizon, were imaged in the water, and Savai'i, in misty outline, seemed tenuous as the clouds.   Generally at noon there was a glare that dulled all save the strongest colours, but towards evening the more subtle tints would awake, emerging as animals that stir at dusk.   Then at night, when amber lights peeped from *fales* and stars from the Milky Way seemed poured into the sea, I would slip across the road and into the black velvet of the water.

Throughout the day on that road, between house and shore, there was constant activity: men with smoothly muscled torsos shining in the sun, women moving with slow and easy grace, children with their only garment worn on the head or shoulders as often as around the hips. Sometimes small naked boys, riding barebacked, would hurtle past the house on their scraggy ponies.   A man with goggles on his forehead would come ashore from the lagoon, a bunch of fish dangling from one hand, a catapult from the other.   Girls would cross the road, their dresses wet and clinging, their hair glistening with sea water.   At almost any hour of the day women would be wading in the lagoon, knee deep, waist deep, probing and picking as they went.   It is man's prerogative to fish in deep water, but the shallows are common to all.

Across the bay the white towers of the cathedral shine as a leading mark to mariners entering the harbour.   A poor harbour it is—as the *Pacific Islands Pilot* remarks: 'It is advisable to put to sea at once upon indication of the approach of a storm.'   The rusting plates of the *Adler*, still conspicuous after nearly sixty years, confirm that opinion, and remind one of the calamitous occasion when H.M.S. *Calliope*, of the seven warships at anchor in the bay, alone escaped disaster.

Once a month the mail-boat calls, immaculately white in the day-time, a nebula of lights at night.   Sometimes a dingy cargo vessel will drop anchor for a few days.   But there is little shipping—the coming or going of even a schooner is an event.

A few days after I returned from Manono, Charlie and
Lavasi'i came to see me. Charlie had decided, at the last
moment, to let his boat go without him and to stay a while
longer in Samoa. Now, he said, Lavasi'i was anxious that
I should pay another visit to his own village, Musumusu,
in Fangaloa Bay. My last visit had been all too short, and
they would prepare great festivities for me if I would
return. He recalled the boat journey from Falefa, where
the road ends some fifteen miles east of Apia, and how, in
the lee of a rocky headland half-way to our destination,
most of the crew had suddenly gone overboard, diving for
clams. Each man carried a short iron bar which he drove
into a partly open shell; then, as the clam closed on the
metal, he gave it a sudden wrench to one side, thereby
tearing the creature from its hold on the rocks. Often as
the men rowed they sang, one song being in special favour.
Charlie translated it for me: 'Adam say to Evi, "I'm in
hell of a fright." Evi say, "Take it easy, boy, we go fetch
some leaves."' The boat was narrow, the sea was rough,
the rowing was erratic—at one moment short strokes in
quick succession, at the next long strokes to a slow
measure; then a rapid increase in speed, ending in a sudden
pause. When they were not singing, the tempo of
the rowing was controlled by falsetto yelps from one
of the nine oarsmen, some of the cries short and sharp
like the barking of a dog, others long drawn like the
howling of a wolf.

We talked, too, of our first evening at Musumusu, when
Lavasi'i had asked if I would like a *fiafia*. I had said that
I thought an early bed was more desirable as we had had
a long day of travel. So after supper three girls came to
make up my bed. But even as they unfolded the mosquito
net they began to *siva*, plucking flowers from the decora-
tions of the *fale* to put behind their ears. A boy who had
been lying unnoticed on the floor picked up his guitar, and,
before there was time to think, the *fale* was full of people,
clapping, singing, and laughing. Whether I liked it or not,
we were having a *fiafia*. The entertainment went on for

a couple of hours with ever-growing enthusiasm, until the climax when, amid acclamation, an elderly woman climbed one of the centre posts and hung head downwards from a beam. When at last the mosquito net was adjusted and I crawled inside, the *fale* was still full of people, and I dropped asleep to the murmur of the guitar.

At Fangaloa the hills rise steeply from the edge of the bay, their great escarpments reducing to insignificance the villages at their feet. The sides of those deeply indented hills are clothed in a richly varied green brocade whose margin is encrusted with the gold of sunlit roofs and whose hem is the silver ribbon of the sand. And as the villages are dwarfed by the hills, so are the hills dwarfed by the clouds that tower above them. Over the rugged contours there is an ever-changing play of light and shade throughout the day until, as the sun sinks, the shadow of the western mountains moves slowly across the bay and creeps upward on the eastern slopes. Then, for a few moments, the Olympian peaks alone are touched with light before they, too, merge into the darkness.

Much as I would have liked to pay a second visit to Fangaloa Bay, I could no longer delay my departure from Samoa. But I thought with regret of the dancing I had seen at Musumusu—the rows of girls sitting cross-legged on mats, motionless, poised; then the tattoo of the drums, and the tap and patter and thud of the dancers' hands on their knees, on their thighs, on the ground, on their own or their neighbours' shoulders. The lines of crossed legs rippled from end to end as the knees, lifting and falling, kept time with the beat. Bodies swaying, flower-decked heads bending and turning, while the rhythm, with faultless delicacy and precision, flowed unbroken from shoulders to finger-tips. There, too, I saw the knife dance; a youth leaping and tumbling as he twirled a long blade, and hurled it, spinning, high into the air; still leaping and tumbling as he caught it again, and sent it once more into the air with added momentum.

My first sight of those mountains at Fangaloa had been

from the boat as we lurched and plunged from wave to wave—great emblems of stability towering above us. My last view of them was when I looked down from a plane and saw below me a Lilliputian landscape scarce raised above the sea.

CHAPTER TWENTY-ONE

T HE EIGHT-HUNDRED-MILE FLIGHT from
Samoa had been uneventful save for a few moments when
the vast dunes of snow-white vapour over which we passed
had parted and, far below, we could see Palmerston Atoll,
its lagoon a pale translucent green as we approached, an
intense electric blue as we looked back, amid the deep
ultramarine of the sea. The plane circled the high volcanic
peaks of Rarotonga, and came to earth on the long strip

cut in the belt of luxuriant vegetation that follows the
shore-line of the island. No sooner had I alighted than
I was aware of incongruity. I was still more aware of it
when I reached the town. Every man was wearing shirt
and trousers, every woman a European frock — there
wasn't a *lavalava* to be seen. And instead of the gentle
'Talofa!' with which I had been greeted everywhere in
Samoa, it was now a crisp 'Good morning' or even a
curt 'Hallo!'

One of the most ignominious acts in a man's life is repeated daily when he puts on his trousers. I know of no garment more detrimental to his natural dignity than those limp tubes into which he inserts his legs. Is there anything in the world more limp than an empty pair of trousers? A toga used as a curtain would still have dignity, a burnous as a blanket would be effective, a string of beads is decorative even on a wall; but of what possible alternate service could a pair of trousers be, except to scare crows? In all the great periods of history, men were not ashamed of their legs. I believe that the decline of civilization set in when they began to wear trousers. Now the fall of it seems imminent since women, too, have taken to them.

The fall of Rarotongan civilization, of which, perhaps, after all, the change of clothing is only a symbol, is certainly almost complete. The people have forsaken the ways of their fathers. Unlike the Samoans, they think that the white man's way of life is better for them than their own: unlike the Samoans, they have abandoned their birthright.

I went with Tupai, one of the old guild of *toungas*, priest-doctors, to Muri on the east coast of the island, to see the fish weirs which are built there in the channel between the mainland and some islets on the reef. Each pair of weirs, he told me, belongs to one family, and they are handed down from father to son as heirlooms. Formerly there were many more of these weirs, but they have not been cared for and, now, while some are so broken that they are useless, others have almost completely disappeared. To-day men prefer food brought in tins from other countries to that which is their natural heritage. After he had shown me how the fish, moving with the tide, were guided by the stone walls, and how inevitable it was that they should go into the traps or nets at the narrow end, we sat down under an ancient ironwood tree and talked of matters which I came to realize were always uppermost in his mind.

Tupai, of middle age, is tall and lean. The intensity of his gaze, and the taut, rather parched skin on his high forehead and acquiline nose called to my mind pictures of early Christian ascetics. At times, as he spoke, he would look at me almost fiercely, then suddenly he would lean back, laughing, and his eyes would disappear into narrow slits. There was an urgency about everything he said: at the same time there was the calmness of long mental discipline. Sometimes he seemed to be looking not at me but through me into another world in which, unconsciously, I existed.

'The white men brought good,' he said, 'but they brought also a whole lot of badness. The most important good thing they brought was the evangelical business. The heathen ways caused a lot of fighting and killing over small things. But before the missionaries came the people had already begun to stop this. In old times,' he said, 'they did not know about clothes. It is more healthy not to wear them, people lived longer without them. When the missionaries arrived there were fourteen thousand people in the Cook Islands; now there are eight thousand. The reason is chiefly because one man lived with three or four wives and he had very many children. As soon as they made the people live as one man one woman, the numbers of the people began to be less. It was better for the race that the men of good blood should have more wives. If they have more wives they have more children than those of common blood.'

'That is the case in many parts of Africa,' I told him. 'The paramount chief of Swaziland, to-day, has seventy-five wives and innumerable children.'

'I think it is wise,' he said.

I agreed with him, providing, I thought to myself, that the numbers are large enough—with only three or four wives there might be jealousy.

'It is good blood that is important for the race,' he said. 'Two trees on the same soil do not have the same fruit. The strong tree has good fruit, the weak tree has bad fruit. Trees need care, people need care. There is no care to-day. There is no control. The people are like a canoe without paddles. They drift with the wind and with the sea. They are not taught the knowledge that belongs to their own people. The old customs have been forgotten. The strong trees are dying. The young trees will not make posts for the new houses.

'Now nothing can be done without money,' he continued. 'In the old days it was the custom of the people that they help each other to do anything. If a man wanted a canoe, every one would help him to build it. Now if a man wants a canoe he has to pay money for the labour. One man by himself cannot make a canoe. If he wishes to build a house it is the same thing. To-day a man does not belong to his people, he belongs to his money.'

The truck that had given us a lift to Muri had now returned and was hooting on the road. As we got up, Tupai kicked aside an empty meat tin that lay in the sand. 'To-day,' he said, 'men do not dig in the earth, they dig in the trading stores.'

He was not returning to town that evening as he was going to visit his daughter who was ill. He thought he could help her. So I travelled alone with Jimmy, the driver, a huge half-caste who filled most of the front seat.

It was a wonder to me that, with the enormous bare feet that protruded from his khaki trousers, he could avoid operating more than one pedal at a time: his naked foot was wider than any ordinary shoe. He said that he was finding it difficult to keep awake, that indeed he had already hit a tree and smashed a headlamp and a mudguard, but he thought he 'd be all right now. He 'd been out after flying-fish the past two nights and hadn't had much sleep. The truck lurched as he spoke, but returned to its course. On dark nights, he told me, they go out in flat-bottomed boats, five men to a boat. One man stands amidships with a flare, another for'ard, and another aft, each with a long-handled scoop net; the other two men row. As the fish fly towards the light the men catch them in the nets. They might get fifty or a hundred in a few hours just outside the reef. . . . His voice trailed off as he spoke, and again the truck did a swerve on the road. 'I think I 'd better have a smoke, keep me awake,' said Jimmy. He stopped the truck with a jerk, gave an enormous yawn, and fell asleep.

As I had no idea how long his slumber might last I decided to leave the truck and continue my journey on foot, but an hour later he overtook me on the road. He was now wide awake and quite recovered. All he had wanted, he said, was five minutes' snooze. That had put him right. The truck was now keeping to the middle of the road. I asked him if he thought the old times were better than the present day. He said he thought 'all times much about same thing. Always someone having a good time, always the other fellow grumbling.'

Before he put me down in the town, Jimmy said that he might be going out again that night. If he did he 'd bring me some fish next day. I said I would like to get one alive, as I wanted to see how the fins worked. He said he 'd fix that.

Just before dawn next morning, after dreaming that, like Hina, I had gone to live in the sea and that a deputation of fish had just waited on me to ask if I would stop my splashing, which they said was continuous and tiresome, I awoke, to find a kerosene tin half filled with water on my bedroom floor with three flying-fish plunging about inside. There was no sign of Jimmy.

On examining the fish, it seemed that their wings, the modified fins, had little capability of an up-and-down movement as in birds. This was a surprise to me, for many times when watching them rise from the water within a few yards of a launch, I had been almost convinced that they did use the fins for flying. Now, however, I got the impression that though the fish might influence the course of their gliding by variations in the set of the fins, they could not use them to increase or even maintain their initial speed on leaving the water. And I was interested to find that in this particular species, the 'wings' when spread have a rich curvature comparable with that of the wings of birds like the partridge and the pheasant, which rise quickly and do not sustain long flights, contrasting with birds like the albatross, whose long tapering wings, with little camber, make it difficult for them to rise quickly from the surface of the water but fit them for soaring over wide spaces of ocean. I noticed, too, that when folded the wings fit into grooves in the sides of the body so as in no way to interfere with the streamlines of the fish.

Rarotonga is the capital island of the Cook group, which extends from the atolls of Manihiki and Penrhyn, more than seven hundred miles to the north, to the volcanic island of Mangaia, over a hundred miles to the south-east. Although small—not more than twenty miles in circumference—it has a grandeur surpassed by few other islands in the Pacific, its central core of mountains rising sharply from a narrow encircling zone of land almost at sea level. Because of the precipitous sides of the mountain peaks, and because of the almost impenetrable thickets that fill the valleys, human activity does not extend far inland from the single road that girdles the island, a road that, shaded by flamboyant trees and flanked with a wealth of flowers, suggests a private avenue rather than a public thoroughfare. Glory after glory of hibiscus, and orange-trees rich in promise; bronze-red blossoms of the tulip-tree, purple sprays of bougainvillea, and purple petals of banana flowers lifting to release whorl after whorl of fingered fruit. Arum lilies growing wild, and in the undergrowth flame-coloured lanterns filled with crimson seeds, and blue flowers like forget-me-nots, creeping under the maroon and yellow sprigs of the lentana. And pervading everywhere the sweet scent of the white tiare blossom.

CHAPTER TWENTY-TWO

A WEEK AFTER the *Tagua* came into port, Captain Matheson gave a party on board. The deck was lit by a lamp hung high in the rigging. Against a background of shrouds and belaying-pins, faces could be seen pencilled in light. Figures sitting on the hatch, on coils of rope or on the deck, were lost in shadows: only an occasional glint of light on eyes or teeth, as a head was lifted in laughter, told of their presence. There were Sam and Rose, Teura, Siaki, Bebe, and many others. Sam, of part Niuean, part Rarotongan parentage, was playing a guitar, his face lit with an exuberant smile. Siaki, from one of the islands near the equator, was sitting beside him, singing, his skin dark from the atoll glare but his features clear-cut as those of a North American Indian. From the corners of his eyes, wide open even when he laughed, wrinkles spread all across his face. Teura, from Tahiti, sweet and gentle, self-effacing for those a few years younger, was playing her accordion. Rose, Sam's wife, also from Tahiti, *petite* and *chic*, leaned towards the music, her forehead puckered in a quizzical frown, her short upper lip curled against her nose in an eager smile. Bebe, languorous, leant against Teura, murmuring the words that Siaki was singing.

The rhythm brought the dancers, one after another, to their feet. From the shadows they moved into the circle of light. Sometimes a girl alone, her hands, her face, her whole body an accompaniment to and interpretation of the song she was singing; sometimes a man and a woman dancing to each other, shoulders, hips, knees in complementary movement, an invitation and an answer, a subtle expression of a sensuous idiom. After a while Siaki took the guitar from Sam, fondling it as a mother might fondle her child. Sam was at no loss; sitting cross-legged, his body swayed to the music, his knees lilted, his toes twitched, his arms and hands in a galloping rhythm urged on the players as a jockey urges his horse.

As the evening wore on most of the guests drifted towards the cabin until, when four bells struck, reminding us that it was two hours past midnight, there were few of the party left on deck.   Some of us rose to go.

'Just a moment,' said the captain.   'There's an old Rarotongan custom to be observed.'   With that, glasses and bottles were put on one side; the table-cloth was thrown into the galley.   'Now, Rose!' said the captain.

Immediately every instrument leaped into life.   Rose began to dance.   From her wedged position on a crowded seat, she swayed to the hula; next moment, without any interruption of the movement, she was standing on the seat; a second later she was on the table.   Small as she was, she could stand upright only when under the sky-light.   The music reached a new pitch of intensity.   Young men, crowded on the floor, began to dance; those who could move in their seats beat time with their hands on the table.   Captain Matheson sat in his chair, smiling.   When Rose had finished, Bebe danced.   When Bebe had finished, Miri took her place.   After Miri there was Tetu, and after Tetu others followed. . . . The trouble when leaving a schooner is that you've got to wait for the swell that lifts the canoe within reach of the ladder.

Next evening I watched the *Tagua* sail.   Slowly, almost imperceptibly, she moved at first, purple against the

147

western sky, her deck crowded with dark figures shouting, waving, gesticulating to their friends on the wharf. Gathering way, she passed between the lines of breakers into the open sea. Then, with her head to the wind, the sails began to rise, flapping and tugging at their ropes. The foresail first, a billowing rectangle, then the triangular staysail and a jib, then aft the great leg-of-mutton mainsail, then for'ard again another jib; finally, as her head was let away and her sails filled, the flying jib like a seagull's wing, catching the evening light.

From time to time, while I waited for another schooner, the *Tiare Taporo*, that was to take me among the outlying Cook Islands, Tupai would come to see me. He liked to talk of other countries, and to hear of people such as those in India who, by rigorous training, can allow themselves to be buried alive for weeks on end without apparent injury, or of Tibetans who by going into a trance are enabled to cover long distances on foot at almost miraculous speed. He chuckled for a long time when, during a discussion of the power of mind over matter, I mentioned the Tibetan saying that 'he who knows how to go about it can live comfortably even in hell.' In the heat of the day we would sit on my lawn in the shade of a *tamanu* tree, but towards evening we would wander along the tracks among the plantations. He told me that when everything is growing specially well, all at the same time, when trees have very many flowers, and fruits begin to show before the natural time of their fruiting, it is a warning that a hurricane may come in two or three months' time. But if the centre shoot of the banana plant, that grows quite straight towards the sky, should bend down—curl over—that is a sure sign that a hurricane will come in two weeks or three weeks or a month. He said, too, that in olden times it was a law that every man must plant at least one *mape* or one *utu* tree, and these trees were taken care of, and when they grew big they were given names. They were very useful to the soil because they held the moisture, and when the hurricanes blew these big trees shook and their roots loosened the soil. The hurricanes are not bad in every way, he said; they carry away all that is weak— the year following a hurricane is always a good year. But now the white man tells the people to cut down the big trees and plant orange-trees. That is no good; where the big trees have been cut down the orange-trees will not grow. On Mitiero, where they leave the oranges to grow wild in the bush, they have the biggest and the sweetest fruit in all the Islands.

Here and there, as we walked, we would pass the sites of ancient ceremonial. Not much to be seen at those places to-day—a circle of stones beside a stream, where sacrificial fires once burned; some fallen slabs, marking a sacred precinct. Most of these places are overgrown with vines and thorny scrub, a few have been desecrated by cultivation. 'Would a white man not mind if a stranger dug in his sacred ground and threw aside the bones of his chiefs?' asked Tupai.

One day I had walked out to that western point of the island, Black Rock, where the dark lava stands as a columned pulpit in the sea. Usually the place is deserted, and on either side of the big rock there are pleasant waters for swimming. On this particular day I found Tupai sitting on the shore with a friend of his, Takarua, an elderly man whose face showed little emotion either when he spoke or as he listened. I gathered that he was one of the senior *toungas*. We chatted for a while before Tupai said to me: 'You have come to the place where the spirits of the dead leave the island.'

'Always from the west?' I asked, remembering what I had heard in Tonga and Samoa.

'Always from the west,' he said. 'Pulotu is to the west.'

'They can be brought back if one has the power,' said Takarua. He spoke so quietly that I could hardly hear him. 'I knew two men whose souls were brought back,' he said. 'They are alive to-day. They began to train for the fire-walking when I began. But it was too hard for them. It is very severe. They died because it was too severe for them. But the *manu aitu* brought back their souls. The *manu aitu* is a very high degree of *tounga*.'

'These things are too difficult for the European,' said Tupai, 'because he uses his head only to have money. He understands only the power that the money can buy. That is not the real power. A *manu aitu* could kill a man only by thinking. If there was any breaking of the law, either a family law or a law of the people, he could call on a spirit of his ancestors, any one of them, to go and fix this thing. Then the spirit would cause sickness, and after sickness there would be death.'

'The *manu aitu* could put a small branch of a tree into the ground and call spirit power into it,' said Takarua. 'Then he say "grow" and it grows, "flower" and it flowers, "give fruit" and it gives fruit. That is power. In olden times, when a chief went into battle he carried only one spear, and one stone for his sling. He knew, when he threw them, that they would be brought back to him by the power of the spirits.'

'I have heard,' I said, 'that when Bishop Selwyn was preaching Christianity to the Arawa tribe of the Maoris in New Zealand, a *tounga* offered to embrace the new faith if the bishop could show the same power that he himself possessed. He then picked up a withered leaf of the *ti* plant, twirled it around his head, and presented it to the bishop, green and alive.'

'The *ti* is a sacred plant,' said Tupai.

'Now I tell you this,' said Takarua. 'If a Maori wish to speak with the spirits he goes along to the *marae*, the sacred place, in the day-time and he plants a piece of the *ti*. It is the plant that belongs with the spirits of the dead; in the fire-walking it was the thing that held the *mana*. Then at night he goes back to the *marae*, and if he is brave enough he plucks up the *ti* plant. And when he has done that he sees all the spirits and he speaks to them, and they give him advice about anything at all. It is just like talking to you or me. I, myself, have done this. The spirits have the forms of men, but at first, when they see you go to get the *ti*, they all change into the forms of animals, like dogs and pigs, and they try to prevent you. Some come towards you and try to fight you, but if you go on they will not harm you. Even before dogs and pigs and horses came to the island, they would be seen, but no one knew what they were. The last thing—it is very frightening— is a big fish mouth, one jaw on the ground, one high above you, and you can feel its breath. But, if you are brave, you walk on into the jaws, and you catch the *ti* plant in your hand. When you do that you have power. You have proved that you are greater than the little things that have tried to frighten you. But it is a big business, and you must have much preparation. It was in 1902 that I began the training for the fire-walking. That took two years. But for the other power it takes much longer.'

I told him of the early Christian saints who wrestled with dragons, and of Buddha fighting with hydra-headed demons whose arms were entwined with venomous serpents and whose mouths spat flames. He said to me: 'All religions are the same when they are alive. It is only when they begin to die that they begin to differ.'

151

CHAPTER TWENTY-THREE

IF ONLY THE COOK had been as efficient as the captain, what a delightful trip we would have had on the *Tiare*, from Rarotonga to Mangaia, and later to Tahiti. But, like Tristram Shandy's father, his mind was not on the job. Dry mash in the morning is wonderful for laying hens, but it does not quicken aesthetic fertility in artists. However, my bunk that overlooked the table in the saloon was beautiful. With the strap of my haversack lashing me to the shackle of the port-hole, I was as steady as a skyscraper in an earthquake. The *Tiare Taporo* is a good schooner, but at times over-sensitive to the wind, like the 'flower of the lime' from which she takes her name.

There must be something in the beams of that vessel, if not in the galley, that inclines a man to the arts. Andy Thomson, the skipper, talks with all the colour of a former captain's paintings. I knew that former captain, Viggo Rasmussen, twenty years ago. I gave him paints and brushes that I didn't need, and he gave me pearls that seemed superfluous to him. I would as soon have a Viggo painting on my wall as an Admiralty chart, and charts are the most significant and stimulating pieces of wall decoration that I know. Viggo's canvases are significant and stimulating, with every sail and every rope doing its duty. Berensen, in his work on the Florentine painters of the Renaissance, describes how Giotto found 'tactile values'— that quality in art which stimulates our sense of touch and makes us conscious of a third dimension. There is no lack of that in those ships and schooners of Viggo's which, under press of sail, ride wide swells of ocean within the narrow boundaries of their frames.

Ten days to Mangaia, calling on the way at Atiu, Mitiero, and Mauke. At Mitiero we stayed only a few hours, but at Atiu and Mauke we were ashore for several days. At each of these islands the nine o'clock curfew was relaxed in honour of the schooner's visit and, night after night, we danced until the early hours of the morning. Strenuous work, those dances. There is no rest; there is no escape. If a man does not invite the woman, a woman very soon invites the man. The floor is of concrete, the hall is crowded, the dancers are zealous, the band is deafening. For the most part the programme consists of foxtrots and waltzes, but an ever-recurring item is the 'Europiana,' a mixture of English barn dance and South Sea hula. You trot a few steps, you clutch your partner and rotate with her, then of a sudden you face each other and waggle your behinds. It is a popular dance and carries with it per-quisites from both civilizations. When, on the morning of the eighth day, wilting, I said to Andy, 'How much more of this?' he said: 'There 'll be a week of it to welcome you on Mangaia.' But he was wrong. It is true there was a welcome, but not with 'profane dancing.'

Atiu, Mauke, Mitiero, and Mangaia are islands whose heights above sea level have been changed many times since their first volcanic cores came into being, and it was during those long periods of slow change that the wide areas of raised coral, now known as the *makatea*, were formed. On Atiu, inside the low sea cliffs, there is a zone

153

of this dead coral around the whole island, in places seventy feet high, in places a thousand yards wide. On Mauke and Mitiero there are similar areas, rather less in extent; but on Mangaia, the largest of the four islands, within a few yards of the shore there is an encircling bastion two hundred feet high, in places more than half a mile in width.

Getting ashore at these islands is not easy. There are no passes through the fringing reef, no sheltered creeks or accommodating harbours. It is 'over the reef' every time —'over' if you are lucky. At Atiu there is one slight break, hardly more than a narrow cleft, in the reef. But even there one must wait for 'the wave,' and, while doing so, there is plenty of time to look down through the clear water into the grottoes below, and to consider at leisure their somewhat self-centred occupants. 'If you're tipped out, swim for the open sea,' I was told. 'There may be a shark or a barracuda about—that's a chance. But if you swim for the reef you'll be smashed—that's a certainty.'

I was lucky. I was never wet above the waist. But time and again I saw canoes and boats overturned and people thrown into the sea. Landing from our schooner one morning, a woman had to swim. On shore during the day she lost her unborn child. When coming on board that same evening, the boat in which she was a passenger again capsized. It was only with hot drinks that we kept her alive that night.

At Atiu and Mitiero I went ashore in the ship's boat, a sturdy craft whose bottom could withstand the fiercest coral; but at Mauke it was in a light shell of a flat-bottomed skiff, not unlike my own *Willow* on the Thames. Perhaps it was that association in my mind that gave an unexpected elation to the landing. A momentary qualm when, on top of a wave, we charged at the reef, men rowing with their utmost effort as if to make destruction doubly sure—then surprise and exhilaration. Incredibly, we were lifted over, and in a frenzy of movement were being rushed towards the shore through a welter of foam. In the boat that followed mine the steersman misjudged the swell. The first wave threw the crew off their balance; the next, following quickly, turned the boat completely over. Passengers and their belongings were thrown into the sea. To most of the people on the shore the incident was hardly more than a momentary excitement. The crowd rushed across the reef flat to be nearer to the fun. Children shrieked with delight. Waves were crashing on the reef relentlessly, while, just beyond, swimmers bobbed about, clutching at any boxes or bundles that floated.

But, unnoticed, three men had launched another boat from the shore. It was only when they met the lines of surf that they were seen. With them there was no waiting for an opportune moment. Their boat was a light one. They charged each wave as it came to meet them—the last of all a big curler. Laughing aloud, they crested that wave, scarce tipping it, almost as a hurdler clears his leap. A shout of applause went up from the onlookers as the boat dropped into the smoother trough beyond. Those in the water were soon picked up, and any baggage that had not sunk was retrieved.

Throughout the day the landing of stores continued, and each boat or canoe that returned to the schooner was laden with sacks of copra. Occasionally a few bags of flour or rice or sugar might get wet on their way to shore, but for the most part less risks were taken with provisions than with passengers. If flour gets wet it is only the outer part

F 155

of each sackful that is spoiled—it seals itself. With rice it is different; it swells and will burst the bag unless quickly spread to dry. With sugar there is no redemption: it just melts away. After a soaking there may be nothing left in a sugar sack but a trace of syrup. Moral: travel, if you can, with sugar. Postscript: before you share a boat with a government official make sure that he is popular.

Pakitoa, a native of Mauke, was an antiquary, specializing in stones. To most of the islanders he was daft. He had a stone that sparkled when the weather was fine; if it was going to rain the stone became dull. He had another, highly polished, with which a *tounga* could staunch the bleeding of a wounded man. It was only necessary to rest the stone on the wound and 'that man ready to fight again two days, perhaps three days.' He had one shaped like a turtle to which men prayed for success before going fishing. 'That stone have much, much *mana*,' he said. He had adzes of all shapes and sizes; one that from an everyday chopping implement could by a half-turn in its socket become an instrument of war; another that by a complete turn could have its cutting edge adjusted for work on the outside or inside of a canoe. He had heavy adzes for felling trees and lighter ones for taking off the bark, and little ones for finishing the canoe, or maybe a dug-out food vessel. He showed me a piece of tapa cloth, which he said was only used at the birth of the first son and for the last child. When I asked how they knew that any particular child would be the last, he said that if a couple decided they wanted no more children, they called together their parents and told them their wish. If the parents agreed to it, then that child would be the last; but if even one of the parents thought otherwise, then the wife would bear more children.

Most important of all in his collection, he had a fish-hook of coral rock whose 'point' was even wider than its shank. 'In olden times,' said Pakitoa, 'you drop down hook into sea and you say prayer to Tangaloa, and Tangaloa give *mana* to hook, and the fish come and they jump on hook.

Now, to-day, you put bait on white man's hook, and you say prayer to white man's god, but no fish come. I think our old god very good. No hard work, no hard prayer. Now we work, work, all the time, and we pray long long

prayer, and sometimes lucky—sometimes not lucky. Me very good Catolico, but me think white god not have much *mana*.'

If the dancing on the island was exhausting, the sight of an occasional tombstone was a tonic. Made of cement, modelled in low relief, and painted in bright colours, they added happy accents to the roadside landscape. The portrait of a young girl holding a Bible in one hand and pressing her other hand to her heart, told us that she knew her Bible by heart. A vivid portrayal of a sinking ship reminded of one who was drowned at sea. There was a full-length portrait of a young man, with his dark hair neatly parted and his features carefully tinted. He wore a black jacket, white trousers and black shoes, a white collar and a crimson tie; his right hand was in his trousers pocket, his left hand behind his back, and, as with many of the other memorials, clusters of flowers filled the vacant spaces of the design. Elsewhere angels with crowns in their hands or cherubs with megaphones to their lips supplied the suitable notes of optimism. Somehow with all of them there was created a sense of continuity:

there was none of that devastating annihilation of white marble.

'What would you like for yourself?' said my host, a cheerful trader. 'I 'll have it put in hand for you.'

'Well,' I said, 'what about a cherub in a green shirt, with a pencil behind one ear and a graver behind the other and he busy with a piece of indiarubber wiping out the smudges on a sheet of white paper?'

'Wouldn't you like any flowers?' he asked.

'Put a little shamrock at my feet,' I said.

CHAPTER TWENTY-FOUR

SURE ENOUGH, there was a welcome for me on Mangaia, though not quite as Andy had predicted. The missionary at Rarotonga knew of the books that Eric Gill had illustrated for me when I owned the Golden Cockerel Press. He knew, too, that Eric had been a relative of the Rev. Wyatt Gill, one of the early missionaries, who had spent the greater part of his ministry on Mangaia. So a message had been sent to the native pastor on Mangaia that a friend of the 'Gilli' family was coming to the island. A few days after my arrival I received the following letter:

'Sir, The Pastor, Dickons and all the Members of the London Missionary Society of Oneroa are inviting you to attend to the Morning Service next Sunday at 9 a.m. and also to be at the Mission House for Meal at 12 noon. We shall be too please if you accept our kind invitation without fail. Please reply before your decision.'

On the next Sunday at 8.55 a.m. the pastor and 'dickons' were waiting outside the church to welcome me. The boys' brigade of the island was paraded there, also. They lined the route, and stood to attention as I approached. Inside the church I was shown to a special pew beside the pulpit. In default of a cushion a pillow from somebody's bed had been supplied, but as the weather was hot I put it on one side, noticing, as I did so, the motto embroidered on its cover: 'Good luck to love.'

After the service I was conducted across the lawn to the veranda of the pastor's house, where I was enthroned among the deacons. Then began a procession of the congregation. From the oldest to the youngest they filed past, each one shaking hands with me and murmuring a welcome. The procession over, delegates from men's councils brought offerings of food—eggs, fish, fruit: delegates from women's committees brought necklaces and flowers. The wife of the king brought me a special hat-band in which shells were woven into a pattern of crowns. All the time there was an accompaniment of song from a choir of men and women seated on the grass before the house.

Then it was announced that *kai* was ready. The pastor led me to an inner chamber where food in every possible profusion was waiting—more than enough for twenty people, and only two of us to deal with it. Women hung wreaths of gardenias around our necks; they brushed away the flies, they fanned us, they anticipated our smallest need. When every button had taken its utmost strain we returned to the veranda, where spokesmen were waiting to tell me of Gillirua—Gill the second; there had been the Rev. George Gill at an earlier date.

'Gillirua, he build church up on *makatea*, top of old coral, same place like your house. And God see this church and He not want church up there; too far away for people. So he say to Gillirua: "What for you go build church up there?" Then he send hurricane, big hurricane, and he blow church flat on ground. And then Gillirua he say: "I think I build new church down by shore." And God say: "That 's right, you build him down on shore." That 's church, where you see him now.'

Another speaker took his turn. 'In old times,' he said, 'people of Mangaia very big men, very thick, very high, high as roof of house. And one day they say to Gillirua, "We very strong men, now we go fight people other islands." So Gillirua very sad, and he say: "You no go fight, fight bad thing; you stay home plant taro." But Mangaia people say: "No, we strong, we very strong." So they go away fight, and while they fight Gillirua pray. Oh, he pray all time—day, night, no sleep, pray, pray, pray. So God listen, and when He listen He say to Gillirua: "O.K., I fix those Mangaia boys." And ever since that time He make all Mangaia people small people, they not grow high any more, no good for fight. That 's how missionaries bring peace.'

When the speaker had finished, the pastor intimated that the party was over. 'Now you may go,' he said.

Already my gifts had preceded me. I climbed the steep ascent to my house on the *makatea*, where I found Roi bustling about. She was worried about her hens. One of them had hatched a mixed brood of three ducklings and nine chicks. 'What you think? Some tuck lay in my hen's bed? No, I no think so. No tuck here. No tuck nowhere here. What you think, my hen meet man tuck? That not make little tuck!'

Roi lived with her husband and family in the house next to mine. Sparse of figure, she was as active in her habits as her more comfortably proportioned neighbours were easy going. It seemed from the first that I presented no more difficulties in the way of adoption than any of her more youthful household. 'You b'long family now, I bring you piece of peeg. When my husband catch fish, I bring you some of him. You b'long family.'

Tom Snow, who managed the trading store in the village, had found the house for me. He seemed also to find everything else I needed. 'The house was there,' he said. 'No good thanking me. 'Twas empty, I didn't do

161

anything.' It was the same with eggs, fish, haunches of goat. The hens were laying, the eggs were there—I might just as well have them. No good thanking him. The fish, too—they'd brought him too many flying-fish, he couldn't help it. And the goat—well, how could he eat a whole goat?

And then there was 'Trenn,' the resident agent. The one thing that bothered Trenn was that he had dispatched his books and his gramophone records to Rarotonga before I arrived. But he was leaving the island; he'd been promoted. However, he had planted extra lettuces and cabbages, and had given instructions that I was to have fresh vegetables sent up to my house every day. In six weeks' housekeeping I don't think my bills came to more than three bags of lollies for the children. Every day someone would appear bringing me a present. It might be one child with a few eggs, or another child with a few pineapples, or a young man with some early limes, or an old woman with a chunk of pork. Apparently there was no compliment about it; I was one of the community and entitled to my share.

The compound, on the highest level of the *makatea*, is about a mile from the shore. After a year of close proximity to the sea it was restful to be in this quiet enclosure, with only a whisper of the buffetings on the reef. On the close-cropped lawn grew breadfruit-trees, orange-trees, coco-nut palms. On all sides there was shelter from the winds. Groves of bananas, kapoks, Norfolk pines, an occasional avocado pear, an occasional coffee bush. Most of the houses were of native design, pleasant shacks of *purau* laths and pandanus thatch.

There was a road at the far side of the compound. Women with bundles of clothes passed to and from the taro swamps where, in the stream, they do their washing. Men with burdens on carrying-poles, others with long knives passed on their way to work, many of them playing ukuleles as they went. Children returned from the bush with large bundles of firewood, or with armfuls of wide

fern leaves with which to cover their family ovens—
scarce one that was not wearing a flower-wreath.

I think that, all in all, as a garland for the neck, I prefer
the white jasmine to frangipane. Jasmine has a gentleness,
a delicacy of perfume. At times, when in profusion, the
frangipane can be overpowering. The crimson *ulas* of wild
ginger petals are handsome in appearance but heavy in
wear. I like a frangipane behind the ear, though for that
position the *tiare*, a white gardenia, is the choice *par
excellence*. It is a charming custom to hand round a bowl
of *tiare* buds with the drinks before a party, as one would
a dish of olives in England. The red hibiscus is, of course,
gorgeous, but its flamboyance is too intense for the pale
European. It needs a setting of ebony hair and honey-
coloured skin. Cubes of dried pineapple rind have a gently
provocative scent, but, like the hibiscus, they are most
satisfactory in dark hair.

Canna flowers are too cumbersome for personal decoration, but they make a happy setting for a bathroom. My
bathroom in Mangaia had a floor of white coral gravel.
Its sides were of *purau* twigs, and all around it grew yellow-
flowered canna plants. Though strictly speaking the

bathroom was mine there were others who made use of it. Occasionally I would see above the near wall a half coconut shell being used to swill water over a tousled head. Occasionally on the inside of the far wall I would glimpse a shadow that emphasized the straightness of the *purau* twigs. There 's no doubt that curves and straight lines do make a splendid opposition in art. The 'Surrender of Breda' by Velasquez in the Prado Gallery, Madrid, and Ucello's 'Rout of San Romano' in the National Gallery, London, are two other notable examples.

But if it is curves that a man is after, the best place for him is far out on the edge of the reef. There, in each oncoming vault of sapphire, he will find all that his soul desireth—wave after wave, unceasing, mounting and rushing, in curves that put a crescent moon to shame, even a crescent Venus. I was very disappointed when I first made closer acquaintance with Venus. Whereas I had expected to find a dazzling sphere, I found a shallow arc, slightly blurred about the inner profile. Venus shines only with reflected light. All her glory is but moonshine.

But to return to earth on Mangaia, there are small snail shells, of exquisite curves, both on the beach and on the rocks inland. With these the women of the island make hat-bands, weaving them into decorative patterns. The shells all look much the same when collected, but boiling with soda, and exposure to the sun, reveal a variety of colours—lemon-yellow, pink, bronze, white, and black. Holes are pierced in them and they are threaded on to a core of kapok. No hat is complete without a band of them.

'Rain time, that 's time you get shells in bush,' said Roi. 'They walk up rocks, you pick 'em off.' She was squatting on the floor of her cookhouse, holding over the fire an old meat tin whose lid had been bent back to grasp a rough wooden handle. In it were shells. As she spoke she peered into the tin, gave the contents a final stir, and then poured them out, a stream of shining gold. Later she would heat some of them again in the same tin, but without water, to bleach them white.

From one thing to another, Roi seemed never to pause. No sooner had she dealt with the shells than she began to open candle-nuts, cracking them between two stones. Then she threaded the white kernels, about twenty at a time, on to the midribs of coco-nut leaflets. 'Now,' she said, putting them aside to dry, 'to-morrow, p'raps next day, they burn good.'

The candle-nut grows luxuriantly on the old coral of Mangaia; the shrubby trees with their apple-green foliage are conspicuous over wide areas. But, personally, for household lighting I prefer the half coco-nut with some coco-nut oil and a wick of kapok twisted round a small stick. It is true that the oil has first to be extracted from other coco-nuts, but the lamp burns with a brighter and less smoky flame than the candle-nuts. On Mangaia the coco-nut lamp was the standard lighting in my kitchen.

One morning I was sitting on my veranda, making a drawing of one of the stone pounders that are used on the island for crushing taro, arrowroot, and other tubers, when a tap at the door made me look up. A child's head was showing above the low rail.

'I brought these for you, Robati,' she said. 'They are for you. It is a present. My father, you know him—the man you talk to on the road, he cough very much—he send them for you.'

I opened the white cloth that she gave me and found five eggs.

'We like to bring you more eggs, but my hen, one day he will come and lay egg, one day he will not come. When he have little chicks he not lay much eggs. When he not have chicks he lay plenty eggs—here, here, here,' pointing as she spoke to my arm-chair, my sketching satchel, and my bed in the inner room.

She folded her hands on the top of the rail, rested her chin on them, and settled down for a talk. 'My name Mata,' she said. 'My father European. He go away, I not see him never. My mother Aitutaki girl, that's where she born me. Then she die, I not see her. My father here—he my feeding father, not my born father.'

Mata's pale skin and the lights in her two thick plaits of hair showed that she was of part-European parentage, but her dark eyes, the short broad nose, and the richly modelled lips told of her native mother. I judged the child to be about twelve years old.

'I live in Aitutaki long time,' she said. 'I got two sisters there, one make me look big, one make me look small. That's where I learn speak English—very big school in Aitutaki. Everybody learn speak English. Here, everybody speak only Maori.'

All the time she was talking she had been taking in the details of my sparsely furnished house.

'Who make your bed?' she asked.

I told her I did so myself.

'Oh, but I am so sorry for you that you make it. I like to make it for you and I like to make the flowers for you, and sweep the floor. I think I cook for you, too,' she added hopefully.

But I declined the offer, explaining that I had a house-boy from the village.

She seemed disappointed at this and, after a little more prattling, she left me. But often during the weeks that followed she would come to see me, bringing some small present, perhaps a few eggs, or a wreath of flowers for my hat, or some sea shells that she had collected on the reef. And sometimes she would bring her ukulele and sit on the lawn before my house and strum while I tried to draw or write.

Then one morning she arrived in a state of suppressed excitement.

'Listen, Robati! Listen my dream,' she said urgently, as she seated herself on the grass at my feet. 'Last night I dream, and I think we on wharf at Aitutaki, you and me, and then schooner come, and we go on board schooner, and captain say he not going Rarotonga, he going New Zealand this time. And you fix with captain for us to go with him New Zealand, and then we sail away in schooner. And I very very happy when I dream that dream, 'cause I like very much go with you New Zealand. And when I wake up I say to my father: "Listen my dream." And he listen. Then he say he very glad for me to go New Zealand with Robati, and he say: "You go tell Robati what you dream, and say I very glad for you go with him and I very happy for you call him ' papa.'"'

She had scarcely finished speaking when her father arrived. He was much better, he said, 'not so coughful to-day.' Yes, he would be very happy for me to take Mata to New Zealand, and he would be very happy for her to call me 'papa.' They both seemed surprised when I demurred and finally excused myself.

On Mangaia more than a third of the children are living with foster parents, some adopted according to Maori custom, others with full European legalities. Usually the arrangement is made soon after birth, but it may occur at any time before the child reaches maturity. The baby may be left with its mother until weaned, but sometimes the adopting parents will take full care of the child from birth, sending it to its mother only to be nursed. Sometimes parents will exchange their children as an expression of goodwill. One man I knew told me that before he was born his mother had arranged with his feeding mother, with whom he now lived, that they would exchange their first babies. So in due course, when he was born, he was handed over. But unfortunately his feeding mother never had a baby of her own, so his real mother had to go without her share of the bargain. But it seems that, for the most part, the custom is linked up with inheritance of land. Land is sacred, permanent; man is only a trustee, a passing tenant. I was told of a dispute about land on another island during which, with a view to calming the discussion, the resident agent quoted a passage from scripture. Immediately the native pastor intervened. 'This is serious,' he said. 'Don't let us drag religion into it.' With marriage, it is the uniting of land that matters, not the uniting of persons. Love comes after marriage, and not, as we know it, marriage after love.

CHAPTER TWENTY-FIVE

EVERYWHERE ON MANGAIA there is a harmony of natural colours. The silver of old thatch is fretted with lavender shadows; the silver of old coral is fretted with violet. The red brown of trodden earth is the red brown of sunlit skins. The golden green of a linnet's plumage is lost among the sunlit leaves.

This is not the linnet that we know in England. It is more like our willow wren, not only in plumage but in its confiding manners. Its song, too, is akin to the warblers. In the early morning when the night airs have quietened and the day breeze is not yet awake, those notes are like a spell, recalling ozier-beds by quiet rivers, and banks of willow herb, loosestrife, and comfrey beside cool streams. I could almost smell the meadow-sweet beside the Thames; I could almost hear the 'gin clear' Wye; I could almost feel the soft mist that in the early hours of morning lingers in the valley of the Lee. I watched a bird day after day among the breadfruit-trees, diving for moths drowsy in the noontide, and I saw it carrying them away, hopping along the ground, pausing to glance from side to side, and I guessed that somewhere among the orange-trees or the avocado pears there was a nest. But I daren't search for it; there were too many young eyes watching me.

There are few song birds in the Polynesian Islands. Even in New Zealand, where the *tuis* and bell birds make chorus in the bush, there is often a silence unknown in English woods. Again and again in New Zealand I was conscious of the lack of birds—whole hillsides of gorse without a feather. But, on the other hand, there were moments of abundant recompense as when, of a sudden and unexpectedly, I saw in numbers birds that are among the rarest at home. Five bitterns together, all of them plain to see in an open marsh; a flock of pied stilts on a mud-flat beside a road. Best of all, known only in New Zealand, four kiwis. And penguins nesting.

The bitterns, separated from each other by a few yards, were ranged along the edge of a bed of reeds in a quiet lake among the hills. For the most part the reeds were dead, but here and there young green was showing; their reflections shone sharp and clear in the unruffled water. When first I crept towards the lake there had seemed to be only one bird, but as I remained quiet, the others of a sudden were there—as it were 'faded in.' The one that first attracted my attention had very dark plumage; it was standing out from its background as a clear silhouette, yet a moment later, by a slight twist of the head, it had melted almost completely into the reeds. Another bird might have been a lichen-covered post in the water, its head stretched upward above its own reflection. A third was standing with its head hunched on its shoulders; a fourth with head thrust to one side, the light glistening on beak and throat as though on faded reeds.

One of the birds was leaning forward, gazing intently into the water, its steel-grey neck clearly defined. Of a sudden it struck, plunging the head below the surface. Up came the head, now with wet plumage a dark-slate purple. The bird raised its beak, jerked a small eel down its throat, ruffled out its feathers and gave itself a shake, then settled down again to quiet observation. A few moments later, almost at its feet, the head of a white-throated shag broke the surface of the water: the bittern crouched as if to strike. A harrier hawk passed low over-head; the bittern took up an aggressive attitude, ready to defend itself. Disturbed by these intruders it waded clumsily to a more secluded position, sinking deep at almost every step, then lifting itself again on to the tangled mat of reeds.

I had only just got the stiffness out of my joints from crouching under cover, when a man who had been working on the land near by spoke to me.

'Have you heard 'em boom at night?' he asked. 'They only do it in the spring, that 's the breeding season.'

'I 've never even seen one alive before,' I said.

'Well,' he said, 'I 'll tell you what I 've seen. It was in the breeding season, too. There was a bittern down in that raupo there, before you, and all of a sudden it rose into the air, making a "quark-quark" as it flew in a big circle all round over the lake—they make that "quark-quark" as well as the booming—and it hadn't got very far before it was joined by another, and then another and another. At last there was thirteen of 'em, and they got up to a terrible height, like a crow does. The first one that went up I thought was the female, and all the others I thought was males. They rose up from different parts of the swamp, and they went round and round, just like the crows. And all the time the cawing noise, the "quark-quark." And then the first one that went up goes off with one of the others, and all the rest drop back into the swamp. Yes,' he said, 'I seen that twice. The other time was in a lagoon not twenty miles from here. I was a kid then, and I didn't know what they was after.'

The stilts were feeding on the marshes just outside Napier, seven thousand acres that only came into being when the earth shook and the heavens seemed to drop, one February morning in 1931. Exquisite birds, always with an air of slight surprise, always with the plaintive cry of a new-born puppy, flicking the mud aside with their upturned bills as they wade among the pools and shingle of the slob land. And then when disturbed, a lovely slow, dream-like glide, with their pink feet trailing behind them, before they settle again a little further from the intruder.

Of kiwis it has been said that they are the most unbird-like of living birds. They have no tails, only vestiges of wings, and feathers that at first glance look like hairs. Their small eyes are rat-like, their powerful legs seem out of all proportion to the size of their bodies.

Those that I saw were in captivity, but as it is rare to see even one of the birds in its natural state the numbers were ample compensation for the circumstances. For the most part the kiwi frequents thick bush, sleeping during the day in a hole dug out of a bank or in a burrow under the roots of some ancient tree, and emerging to feed only at night. Owing to the destruction of natural bush and the ravaging of imported animals such as the cat and weasel, the numbers of the kiwi diminished to an alarming extent, but to-day the bird is protected by law and there seems every chance that it may survive extinction. It is now illegal to keep any of these birds in captivity, but a special Act of Parliament has enabled Mr. Frank Robson, curator of the Acclimatization Farm near Napier, to do so. It is believed that his young birds are the only ones ever bred in captivity.

'No bigger than a hen and lays an egg a pound in weight,' said Mr. Robson. 'And the male does all the sitting. Seventy-five days it takes him. And the female hardly ever comes near him all that time, except to lay another egg after he 's been on the first one a month—means he 's got to go on sitting for another month after the first chick is hatched. He loses about two pounds in weight while he 's sitting, and that 's a lot for a bird of five pounds. Only comes off the nest an odd time at night to pick a few worms. Worms is what they mostly eat, but they like maggots and grubs, and I 've seen 'em eat a few berries, too, and I 've seen 'em run the bill into a cabbage and pick out the centre part. The bill is very tough; they drive it into the ground after the worms.'

As he was telling me this, Mr. Robson pointed to the soil in the run, which was perforated in all directions.

'Oh, but the old man looks a real picture on the nest,

just a ball of feathers,' continued Mr. Robson. 'He gets very savage if any one disturbs him. Sometimes he will hiss and snarl like a cat, and if you touch him he will strike at you with his foot. He's quick, too, and that spur will give you a nasty tear.'

He took me to a box under a tree where the hen was sleeping. 'Look at her, with her bill tucked under her little bit of a wing,' he said. Then he picked up the sleeping bird. 'And look at that leg,' he said; 'stronger than a turkey's. And the beak—the nostrils right at the tip. That doesn't happen in any other bird. All the time they're feeding they have to keep blowing the dirt out of their nostrils: you can hear them making a sniff, sniff as they go along.'

I remarked on the small eye of the bird. 'Sight is very bad,' he said. 'They can hardly see at all in the day-time, but wonderful hearing and smell. When the youngsters get a few yards away from him the old man has to put his bill to the ground and follow them by scent. It's the male that looks after the youngsters all the time: they never go near the female.'

I referred to the fact that apart from laying the eggs the hen played little part in the domestic economy. 'The only time she shows any interest,' said Mr. Robson, 'is when the chick is near hatching. Then she'll go along to the box and tap it all round with her bill, and the male will tap an answer from inside. I timed her one night when the egg was chipping, and she tapped every two and a half minutes.'

On the cliffs of Otago the yellow-eyed penguins nest, not, as one might expect, on rocky ledges, but amid patches of native bush perhaps half a mile inshore. Coming from the sea they flop and flap in the shallow water, running before the wavelets, knocked down when overtaken. Once above the water-line they stand, sedate and dignified, looking back at their companions still in the water, as if surprised at their clumsy antics. Then, in single file, solemnly, their heads held high, they march across the sand to the boulder fringe below the cliff face. Once again their dignity is shaken as they hop and slither and jump and fall among the large uneven stones. But on reaching the grassy verge of the cliff they resume their dignified demeanour. For a while they rest, standing erect; then, in procession, following accustomed tracks, they climb the cliff, waddling, jumping, clambering towards the nesting sites among the tangle of nettles, fallen branches, and tree-trunks.

A bird on the nest shows a mottled blue-and-silver back, dappled as a guinea-hen, shining as a mackerel, while its large golden eyes weep tears of anxiousness as strangers approach.

Other birds come ashore through heavy seas on to a rocky foreshore. They seem impervious to the battering of the waves. One moment they are thrown about, as if helpless, in the surf; the next, under water, they are swimming at amazing speed, in complete mastery of the element. Then of a sudden they appear to be cast ashore, and, as unexpectedly, are waddling and jumping over the rocks towards a climb that would be formidable even for a man.

CHAPTER TWENTY-SIX

ALL THE TIME that I was on Mangaia I had a feeling of instability, a feeling that at any moment the island might sink below the sea. The forms, not only of the great barrier wall but of the individual fractions of that rock, are so dramatic that one cannot but imagine them to be the result of some sudden cataclysm, that the jagged edges of the cliffs can only have been rent by some monstrous explosion.   There is a feeling, too, of unreality, that the island has been enchanted into being.   And even when one knows that all is the result of age-long natural growth, the fantasy of the supernatural remains.   Every cave is a magician's cave, every ascent or descent in the rock is a stairway to or from the dwelling-place of a sorcerer, hag, or warlock.   Anything may change at any moment, the swamps may turn to cataracts, the rocks dissolve to dust, the red mountainous core may become a sea of flame.   And when one walks on those high mountain ridges there is a sensation of being in a primeval world. It seems as if the red powdery soil has but just drained itself of the sea, and that the salt still permeates it, rendering it barren to all but a few small struggling ferns.   Animal life has scarcely appeared, no mammal grazes, no bird makes its nest; only an occasional lizard to enhance the illusion of a prehistoric time.

The narrow tracks that follow the crests of the hills might once have been the tracks across spongy ooze, scarcely above sea level.   Through countless generations primitive man felt safety in the footpaths of his parents, the paths that all the time were being lifted further from the sea.   There is on the island of Mitiero to-day a lake whose sulphurous margins yield, as a bog, to human feet.   Only by narrow tracks—tracks that may one day crest a mountain —can the edge of that lake be reached.

But it is in the caves that one is most aware of the phantasmic nature of the island.   Huge caverns, their ceilings dripping stone.   Dripping, all the time dripping. Monstrous pillars, in semi-human forms, weep through a thousand generations.   Gnome-like bodies lie contorted on the floor.   Gorgon masks glare from the aisles.   Gargoyle faces grin from the calloused ceilings.   From an opening on the western face of the *makatea* one looks across the valley, two hundred feet below, to the mountain ridges that rise so abruptly from the swamps.

For a while I entertained the idea of spending a night alone in one of the caves.   I pictured to myself the quiet of evening up there, with the warm sunset colours glowing from the sculptured pillars. The sun would be shining into the mouth of the cave, and the great fangs that hang from the upper lip would cast curious shadows on the warty coruscated roof. The sun would set behind the peaks of Rangimotia, turning its red earth to purple, and mauve shadows would spread across the cool green taro swamps in the valley, far below. Brown specks in the streams would be families at their evening bath, white crescents in the sky would be terns wheeling. And then before dawn, while the cave was still dark, the western sky would glow with reflected sunrise and the red hills would be aflame, and deep blue shadows would fill the valley. Perhaps there would be an early morning mist, and then, aloof, I would exist in an eyrie high above the clouds.

But between dusk and dawn there would be night. I suddenly thought of that—black night with no moon. I could feel the damp chill. I could hear the stalactites ringing like bells if touched. I could hear the hoarse chuckle of the night bird. There would be other noises, too, unrecognizable in the darkness. There might be rats, hundreds of them, scurrying among those petrified entrails. It is certain that goats inhabit those terraces at night: in the dark I suppose their white bodies would show faintly luminous, and I would hear their pattering, galloping hooves, and probably they would let out a sudden whinny which would echo in my spine. And as the night wore on strange smells would rise; even in daylight there is an unaccountable odour of horses. It isn't that I get nervous. It's just that I go cold and clammy all over.

It is only a short while since vanquished tribes lived in these caves. To-day, therein, hunted men can still find sanctuary. Many of the caves in ancient times were the burying places of the people; to-day they are shrines. For those few people who know or are guided to the right entrances there are to be found vast mausoleums not only of human bones but of tribal relics. But they are carefully guarded, they are *tabu*. In one of the larger of these caves is a mighty spear, thirty feet in length and as thick as a man's wrist. It belonged to the hero Kanune who stood eight feet high. Kanune would wait until a battle was at its height before joining the fray, then rushing in he would impale three of the enemy at one thrust. Not content with that he would then rest the butt of the spear on the ground and, raising its head aloft, exhibit his writhing victims. Small wonder that he struck terror into the hearts of his enemies; small wonder that his name has become legendary.

It was dusk when they brought the sick woman back to the compound. Three days earlier, when native treatment had failed, they had taken her to the hospital. But by then it was too late; and now, on a white-covered litter, followed by her mother and a few other womenfolk, she was carried to her home by four men, a silent procession among the dark trees. A light was flickering through the slatted walls of her house. A murmur of voices could be heard from within. In the gloom one could see ghostly figures entering and leaving the house. It was rumoured that the wise man had come to resume his treatment, that the pastor had come to pray. Perhaps she would live after all.

But a few hours later I was awakened by the high wailing of a woman in grief. Other voices could be heard, talking excitedly in low tones. Footsteps came and went. There was no more quiet that night. Frequently and regularly that high-pitched cry of lamentation could be heard above all other sounds.

It was scarcely dawn when people from the neighbourhood began to arrive, women in freshly laundered white dresses, children in stiffly starched white shirts. The women entered the house by one door, and after a few minutes came out by the other. The children crowded at the doors, peering into the darkness. As each woman emerged she joined a group of others who, sitting on the grass, were talking quietly, leaning towards one another to whisper; nodding, with glances towards the house. Presently the old mother appeared, thin and grey, wrapped in a dingy sheet. She crouched low among the women, bowed her head to her knees and keened, rocking her body from side to side.

But as the hours passed a change came over the scene. The women no longer sat idle, talking. Everywhere there was a bustle and activity. Solemnity had given way to anticipation. Men arrived with baskets of taro, which they spilled in heaps on the grass. They brought fresh palm fronds which the women split and wove into baskets. They brought banana leaves which the women spread on the ground. Voices were no longer subdued. Occasionally one could hear laughter. Even the notes of a ukulele became audible. Then a horrible squealing of pigs in the nearby bush told of the main interest of the day. Presently men appeared carrying the dead animals on their shoulders. Now voices and laughter grew louder. The men dropped their burdens to the ground and chopped at them with their long knives.

The sight of red meat and blood had a tonic effect, the tempo of the party increased. Jokes were bandied. The ukulele became louder; a woman was singing to it, another was dancing. Children, naked and half naked, ran among the workers, picking up and brandishing the knives that momentarily had been laid down. Carcasses were split, limbs torn asunder. The 'lawn' became a shambles, and, as the bones were cracked and the joints disintegrated, each pile of taro received its portion of dripping meat. The dead woman was forgotten; even the mother had ceased to weep. She sat watching, quietly, sometimes smiling.

The women of the house had been too excited to think of dress. In tattered rags they busied themselves, now here, now there. When on one of them the last shreds of an upper garment fell apart, she continued in her work.

naked to the waist. As, with a haunch of dripping flesh in either hand, she danced across the scene, she might have been a maenad in her fury.

Blood and flesh and grinning heads of sacrificial pigs, and men and women lustful for meat.

CHAPTER TWENTY-SEVEN

DURING MY STAY on Mangaia I increased the white population by twenty per cent. This might seem an alarming statement if I did not add that before my arrival there had been only four Europeans—my presence added a fifth. But it leads me to the subject of 'morals.' I don't think there is more than a ha'p'orth of difference between the young people of Polynesia and the young people of white races in that respect. It is just that in the Pacific they are a little more honest about it all. A higher proportion of births outside of matrimony does not prove more immorality; in England that proportion is far higher in the rural districts than in the cities, but the standard of behaviour is not lower.

One often reads of 'the thieving propensities of the natives,' and it is true that here and there it may be wise to turn the key of one's suit-case, but in how many places in Europe could one leave possessions lying about if the houses were open? I stayed in a house in Tahiti for two months, and whether I was at home or abroad it was always open. It was, indeed, impossible to shut it, for there was nothing but blinds on one side. If I went away for a few days, as I often did, I left all my belongings exactly as if I had been there to stand guard over them, and nothing was ever touched. Those who talk about the pilfering of natives should discuss souvenir hunting with the pursers of ocean-going ships, especially of those which carry wealthy passengers.

And while I am being belligerent, a word on so-called 'unprovoked attacks.' I believe that there have been few acts of aggression by the natives of the Pacific islands against visiting white men unless those same white visitors or their predecessors have provided ample justification. As an instance of the complete callousness with which some of the early voyagers treated the natives, we have an account by the Dutch navigator, Schouten, who tells us how, when near the island of Niau-tobutabu, to the north of Tonga, he met a canoe in which were about a dozen men as well as eight women and three children at the breast. As the canoe did not stop at his signal (which they probably did not understand) he fired on them four volleys from his muskets. He consoles himself by saying that 'the wounds being from hail shot were not very deep.' The murder of the missionary, John Williams, in the New Hebrides followed the wanton killing of several natives by sandal-wood traders. The massacre at Tutuila of eleven of the crew of *La Pérouse* occurred after a native had been shot by the white men for a trivial offence. The attack on Captain Cook by the Niue Islanders was made because they were already suffering from an epidemic brought by an earlier ship and feared the introduction of another plague.

Even Captain Cook's men were not entirely free from blame. In his journal, describing his stay in Tahiti, he writes: 'I sent the boat on shore with an officer to get ballast for the ship, and not immediately finding stones convenient for the purpose, he began to pull down some part of an enclosure where they deposited the bones of their dead: this the Indian violently opposed, and . . . would not suffer it.'

Finally, while on this subject, if in the past an occasional ship when wrecked on a reef was plundered, we need not go beyond the coast of Cornwall, at the same period, to find parallel behaviour.

Evening on Mangaia: banana leaves motionless, their frayed banners profiled against the sky, their young unbroken leaves bright against the darker green of the citrus-trees. As the light fades the jungle creeps closer: it becomes a dark backcloth for a scarce-lit stage on which figures in moth-white dresses come and go. Late at night, when old men cough or children cry, warm lights flare through the *purau* slats.

There was always some sound in the compound, yet

there was always a sense of quiet. At midnight I might hear the snorting of a horse as he grazed beside the house. Queer horses these on Mangaia; Tom Snow told me that he had to train his animal to eat oats by mixing them, a little at a time, with a mash of pawpaws. Or there might be a piglet routing under my veranda, or merely the thud of a falling coco-nut or the swish of a dead frond on its way to earth. At four o'clock every morning I was awakened by a conch shell being blown to announce that the bread oven had been opened. About the same time the cocks of the island would commence their crescendo of crowing. Soon after daylight the hand drums would be

beaten to call the children to school. Early in the fore-noon the official crier might be busy with his drum, announcing tidings of general interest. And, always, there were children who, for hours on end, in tranced concentration, would beat out rhythms of their own, with sticks on empty coco-nuts or with just sticks on sticks. And if there was silence from the vertebrates, there would be the hum of insects, or there might be a shower of rain stampeding up the valley, or the rain-like patter of palm fronds in the wind.

The morning came when the beating of the drum announced that a schooner had been sighted from the *makatea*, the *Tiare* which was to take me from Mangaia. It was expected that she would be in by noon. They said that the reef was not good. On those islands without an anchorage the state of the reef is more important than the weather overhead. Often, indeed, your greeting to a friend may be 'Good reef!' instead of 'Good morning!' or 'Bad reef!' instead of 'Windy day!' But the fact that the reef might not be 'workable' that day didn't worry Tom Snow. He arrived at my house with a truck, loaded my belongings into it, and said that I was staying with him till the schooner sailed—the longer the better.

The *Tiare* was still low on the horizon when we got down to Tom's house, and as we sat watching her we wondered if she would 'make it' that day, beating up against the wind. But, early in the evening, Andy was ashore.

'Come on! No time to wait. Reef's bad, and it's getting worse. Glass is low—there's something about.'

'Talking of glasses——' said Tom.

'Well—just one for the reef. Head wind all the way. Carried away a jib in a squall. Here goes—"Down the hatch!" It's late in the year, glad when we get up north —north of fifteen south.'

'Did you bring all my stores?' asked Tom. 'Shan't see another schooner for five months.'

'Brought you everything,' said Andy. 'Plenty of castor oil and kerosene, and there's a sack of potatoes for yourself and a sack of oats for your horse, and a case of rum for Christmas, and the mail, and a bundle of papers that takes you up to three months ago. What's that? I can't row with one oar? I believe you're right. Well— "Bottoms up!"'

The king and the pastor and the 'dickons' had come to see me off. Roi was there, too, with a last present of a hat-band and a floor mat. Little Mata, without speaking, put a handkerchief with four eggs in it into my hand. She had tears in her eyes because I could not take her to New Zealand. There were hanks of bananas, crates of pineapples, and a sack of limes for me, but who they were from it was impossible to find out. They were piled in the boat awaiting our departure. 'Take those *leis* off your neck,' said Andy, as the boat was pushed off. 'You can't swim in those.'

But despite appearances there was no swimming. We got on board without upset.

Early next morning we reached Mauke, and after a few hours ashore while stores were being landed we sailed for Atiu. Again a few hours to land stores and then, with the

wind on our beam, to Aitutaki, the last of the southern
group, some hundred miles to the west. According to
tradition Aitutaki was first peopled by a chief, Re-enua,
who, with his four wives, four brothers, and twenty un-
married women of high rank, sailed in his canoe from
Havaiki, the ancestral homeland of the Polynesian people.
Many centuries later the island became known to Europeans
when on 11th April 1789 Captain Bligh, with his cargo
of '1015 beautiful Breadfruit Plants and many Fruit kind,
in all 774 Pots, 39 Tubs and 24 Boxes,' rediscovered it.

Aitutaki is a mixture of atoll and high island, having
on the south-east a lagoon six miles wide and on the west
a ridge of hills nearly four hundred feet high. Bligh was
unable to land owing to the 'prodigious Surf,' though
much to his surprise four men in a canoe, around which
'the sea broke dreadfully,' did manage to visit his ship.
If he had reached the island in 1946, as we did, he would
have had no difficulty in landing, for a fast motor launch
would have come from the shore and taken him at surprising speed through a deep passage that had been blasted
in the reef. He could have stepped from the launch on
to an elegant pier without even taking the shine from his
silver-buckled shoes, and if with a premonition of im-
pending events he had preferred a quicker journey to the
East Indies than, eventually, he was compelled to make,
he might well have found an aeroplane on the air-strip
ready to take him on the first step of that journey, Aitutaki
being the place of call between Samoa and Rarotonga.
'It's terrible,' said a white resident to me. 'There's a
plane comes in every fortnight. The noise is deafening,
and every one starts rushing around and fussing. I can't
stand it, it's getting on my nerves. I'm going back to
Mangaia.'

The moment of arrival at any new island is a good one,
but I often think that the moment of departure is even
better. Arrival is exciting, stimulating, but it is usually
early in the day and there are problems to be faced. Departure is, as often, towards evening—the work of the day

is over, the heat of the day is spent. Farewells have been said; the last canoe-load of visitors has left the ship's side. One can relax. Soon the sails are set, and from the after-deck one watches the island recede in the evening light. The ship and its crew and its passengers have become once more an entity. There is a feeling of fellowship, of detach-ment from the rest of the world. Then is the time when Andy likes to talk. He comes astern, climbs on to the old store-chest abaft the wheel-box, and, sitting cross-legged, dispenses wisdom. Together we 'grow profound.' We 'rectify the world,' we 'tranquillize the nations.' We agree with all great thinkers who do not disagree with us.

'One of the troubles,' said Andy, 'is that we all think we're as good as the fellow above us, but none will admit that he's no better than the fellow below him. Yes, and there's some people wonder what use they can be to the world, and others wonder what use the world can be to them.'

And when the sun has gone down in a tumult of flame, we watch Scorpio and Orion and the Pleiades wake up and blink, same as they've waked up and blinked for a million years; and the only sounds are the creaking of a rope and the hiss of a following wave.

'A neighbour of mine was a deacon,' said Andy one evening, 'and he certainly was a bit of a thief. You never

knew when he wouldn't steal a chicken or two. But there, if he hadn't been a deacon he'd probably have stolen a pig. No, there's nothing wrong with the missionaries, only they won't agree among themselves. While they've been disputing about a footpath to heaven, Hollywood has opened a motor road in the opposite direction. But I reckon they done the hell of a lot of good. Wasn't it that fellow Darwin who said: "How'd you like to be wrecked on an island the missionaries hadn't been on?" I guess he was about right.'

As we neared Manihiki Andy told me of a small black-and-white striped fish that inhabits those waters. 'Well, it's about February, I suppose, when this little fish starts to look around. He begins to poke among the stones, to dig himself a sort of little cave, a nest you might say, with a couple o' neat little doors, one back and one front. And those black and white stripes on him—well, the black gets blacker and the white gets whiter, and he hangs around getting all worked up, and one day a bunch of half a dozen little female fish come along and have a look, and the old man bristles up. All his colours come brighter than ever and he sidles up to one of the girls, and he says: "Come along, sweetheart, come and have a look at my flat, two doors and all conveniences!" And she goes along with him and he shows her around, and—well, I don't know just exactly how he does it but, somehow, he persuades her to stay.'

A white tern overhead cast its shadow on the deck. 'Look up from the shadow and you 'll see silver wings,' said Andy. 'Wherever you live,' he went on, 'whatever the climate, there 's always some drawback. Hurricanes and tidal waves in the islands; floods and soil erosion on the mainland. You live in the tropics and you lose your nose by leprosy; you live in Alaska and you lose it by frostbite. You go to California where there 's a perfect climate, and what do you find there? A lot of religious cranks who drive you nuts—say the world 's coming to an end and taking the climate with it.'

CHAPTER TWENTY-EIGHT

CHRISTMAS DAY on the schooner was uneventful for every one on board but the poor pig. That night we dined on fresh pork. Next day we reached Manihiki.

As the ship coasted the reef we could see heavy purple clouds on the far side of the atoll. The lagoon showed milky white. It was a question of whether or not we would get ashore before the rain came down. But after a somewhat exhilarating reef crossing we did reach land without a wetting, and hurrying to a nearby house we took refuge from the storm that almost immediately broke over our heads. As we sheltered I could hear through the rattle of rain on the iron roof an occasional beating of drums. Yes, I was told, Christmas festivities were still going on. There would be dancing that afternoon. Why, of course they 'd like me to see it; it would begin at any moment.

A man threw a canvas sheet over my shoulders, another gave me a banana leaf to cover my head, and with the two of them leading I dodged among the dripping breadfruit-trees to the village hall where the performance was to take place.

Instead of dancing I found a religious service in progress, with the pastor standing among his congregation, leading them in prayer and hymn-singing. But that didn't last long; it was merely the orthodox prelude to the dance. Then the company moved from indoors to the wide veranda that looked on to the open sandy space that was to be the scene of action. The drums had already been assembled, one a big double-faced one hanging from a rafter, two of carved wood standing on the floor. One of these had a tympan of goat skin, the other—the better one, I was told—of shark skin. It was a very old one, with its own name,

Rakomeramera, and held in great honour. Eight wooden drums and a kerosene tin completed the orchestra.

The rain, now at its heaviest, did not deter the dancers; a crash of drums brought them running into the open. Men and women, they formed up in four rows, seven in each row. Over their white European clothes they wore girdles of leaves, on their heads were wreaths of oleander blossom.

Another crash of drums and the dance began. The women, with shoulders and feet almost motionless, swung their hips violently from side to side. The men, with every joint of their legs and arms loose and flexible, danced in rapid staccato phrases, faster and faster with the increasing tempo of the drums. The noise became deafening; at each successive moment a higher peak of emphasis was reached. Unable to resist the excitement, elderly women rushed in from the crowd and joined the performers. At one side, under a tree, three naked children, their bodies shining in the rain, were equally engrossed in their own version of the dance. And on the packed veranda the onlookers swayed and clapped and stamped in sympathy with the dancers.

The drums ceased abruptly. As suddenly, the dancers were still. Not a muscle quivered. That is part of the art—to rise to an intensity of disciplined abandon, and then to finish, clean-cut, without a tremor.

There was a short pause before the noise began again and another group of dancers appeared. With tireless vigour and enthusiasm the drummers hammered out the rhythm, working up to frenzied climaxes, while the flower-wreaths slipped from their heads and the sweat from their exertions glistened on their skins. The rain poured and poured upon the dancers; their clothes clung closer to their bodies, the water streamed from them, their feet churned up the grey sand now pooled with water. But the downpour seemed only to exhilarate them, to incite them to greater efforts.

So it went on, each dance finishing with unerring

precision, and as each group of performers, dripping and exhausted, trooped from the scene it was rarely that a few of the women could withhold a last unbridled gesture—a final, provocative, almost derisive pelvic flourish.

The pastor stood up. Every one gathered round him, the dancers still panting from their exertions. They bowed their heads while he prayed, they lifted up their voices when he gave them the opening words of a hymn. Then the party was over.

I had not expected to spend more than one night at Manihiki, but the swell on the reef increased, and the following day, though the sky was clear, there was no possibility of getting the stores ashore. For another twenty-four hours the schooner lay off and on, waiting for the sea to subside; but at last Andy decided that, the wind being where it was, the reef at Rakahanga, an atoll twenty-five miles to the north and our next isle of call, might be easier to work. So away went the schooner, leaving me marooned until such time as she should reappear.

My host, Dan Ellis, was a patriarchal figure, as mighty in height and strength as he was gentle in manner and speech. He had assumed from the first that I would stay with him, and quickly had a house made ready for my use. This house, originally a store, was built on a pier of coral rock that jutted into the lagoon. 'You have a garden all around you with plenty of flowers in it,' said Dan, pointing to the fish that swam close by in the water. 'Not much food on the island till the stores come ashore,' he added, 'but I guess we find something.'

Being Christmas time, there was neither pearl-shell fishing nor copra-making, but I found no lack of diversion. The morning after my arrival I sat with Dan on the shady side of my house, watching the outrigger canoes with their triangular sails skimming across the lagoon, and the small cutters with their white hulls and sails reflecting the colour of the water as they raced from islet to islet. Presently a boy swam close to the pier, pushing before him a log of wood on which was balanced a fishing-rod. Under the log a basket was fastened, and into this the boy dropped the small fish as he caught them. A little further from the shore a man sat in a canoe, cleaning pearl shell. After a cursory search for pearls he threw the flesh overboard; then with a heavy knife he chipped away the coral encrustations from the outside of the shell.

Pearls are so rare in these waters that they are thought of merely as perquisites. It is shell by the ton that gains regular money. When it is first brought in from the diving grounds, it is dumped into shallow water near the shore, there to await a time, maybe six months or a year ahead, when the owner feels inclined to clean it. 'Money in the bank,' said Dan.

While we were talking a large golden leaf drifted past in the water. In its shelter were half a dozen small blue fish nibbling at a fragment of coco-nut. Near by cruised a shoal of mouse-grey fish, their black fins speckling the water like frog spawn in a pond. They vanished suddenly when the tawny bodies of three sand sharks appeared in sight. Each shark had its pilot swimming close before its nose—so close that the shark might have been holding the tip of the small fish's tail in its mouth. One shark had four of these fish, each about four inches long, striped with yellow and black like a wasp, swimming in line abreast, and all the time moving as though held together by some invisible wire.

'Those sharks don't bite,' said Dan. 'If you go swim in the lagoon they run away quick. No biting sharks in Manihiki lagoon. But plenty in Penrhyn.'

Two days before the end of the year Ben, Dan's brother, who lives on the far side of the lagoon, sent his cutter to fetch me. No sooner had I reached his house than he produced a bottle of wine that in flavour and appearance was not unlike a heavy, sweet Madeira.

'Mead,' said Ben. 'My father came from Yorkshire. That's where he learn to make it. That's where he learn to make the boats, too. It was my father teach the Manihiki men how to make boats. That cutter you sail in to-day is fifty-three years old. My father built every bit of it himself. When the hurricane came along in 1914—that was the year before the old man died—it smashed up the boat. But I built it again. It's the same boat, I reckon.'

He filled my glass a second time, and while I drank he copied the recipe for me from an ancient leather-bound chronicle:

'To make 2 gallons Mead

Water	11 pints
Honey	4 „
Tartaric Acid	7 grammes
Pollen	7 „
Subnitrate of Bismuth	1 gramme

'Put the honey into a two-gallon jar with the water. Add the tartaric acid and subnitrate. Mix the pollen with a little water and add it to the rest. Mix all together. Then place a piece of cotton over the mouth of the jar and tie up so that the air can get out. When the bubbles stop rising, pour in a cup of boiling water and fix a good cork. Put jar in a warm place. When the scum rises and then sinks to the bottom, pour the liquid into pint bottles. Leave it if you can for one or two years before drinking, but it is all right after two or three months.'

As he was writing this down I thought of the early missionaries who, when they first came to Manihiki, appointed a vigilance committee in each village to watch over the morals of the people. Any member of those committees could stop a man on the road and tell him to 'blow.' According to the fragrance of the ensuing breeze he decided whether or not the man had been drinking.

If he considered that his victim was guilty he imposed a summary fine; and there was no appeal. As half the fine was divided among the committee, there was no lack of zeal among its members.

Even more stringent was the treatment of other delinquents. Any one suspected of departure from the narrow path—normally fairly wide in Polynesia—was put in the stocks to await trial. If caught on a Saturday evening the culprit had to remain in public bondage till Monday morning, lest the Sabbath be desecrated by a trial. A woman found guilty was not only fined but drummed out of the village. The girls of the island, however, soon learned how to counter that notion. The more the drums beat the more they laughed. Ridicule restored to them their rights.

After lunch Ben and I wandered through the village, glancing at the stores of shell neatly piled to await the first schooner after the hurricane season. We looked also at the village fish trap, an elaborate maze of pools, their walls just breaking the surface of the lagoon. Unlike the chevron weirs at Rarotonga, which need their owners' presence when the fish are running, these formed a labyrinth from which at any time there could be little chance of escape. Once a fish was there he must perforce wait till called for.

Ben had invited me to remain with him for the New Year celebrations, but owing to uncertainty about the schooner's return I deemed it wiser not to stay. I would certainly have had a more festive time if I had stayed for, early on New Year's Eve, in Dan's village, an old man died, and throughout the day there was wailing and moaning, a cacophany of noise that only ceased when, late in the afternoon, the funeral was over.

On account of the death there was no gaiety in the village that night, and so in the light of the half-moon I sat on my veranda and thought of New Year's Eve at home. Gin and coco-nut milk I was drinking—there was no alternative. If gin was scarce, drinking water was scarcer. Names like Roederer and Mouton-Rothschild and Graham floated through my mind. I thought of men in evening dress: I had a couple of yards of cotton around my middle. I thought of women with pearl necklaces; on my table was a large blister pearl that Dan had given me as a New Year's gift.

Half an hour before midnight Dan called for me to go with him to church. The service had begun when we entered the building, but the pastor interrupted his ministrations to shake hands with me and thank me for coming. He then borrowed my watch, saying that his alarm-clock was not reliable. Neither was my watch. But somewhere about midnight the New Year was ushered in with ringing of bells and much embracing. I escaped to my house and changed again into my cotton *pareu*.

By now the wind had dropped completely. Every star was clearly reflected in the lagoon. The moon was low behind the palms. I thought of the people who, in stuffy clothes, were welcoming the New Year in crowded buildings. Standing on the veranda, I dropped my *pareu* and dived into the lagoon, to meet the New Year among the reflected stars.

CHAPTER TWENTY-NINE

EVENTUALLY THE SCHOONER came back.
Day after day we had searched for sight of a sail. But day
after day the heavy sea was pounding on the reef. It
would not have made any difference if she had come back;
we couldn't have crossed the reef and they couldn't have
come ashore. 'Andy knows,' said Dan, and sure enough
on the first fine morning that the sea had eased there was
the schooner waiting to unload and load.

Andy seems to know every yard of that ocean. To most
people its state would be as unpredictable as the laying
habits of a cuckoo. Yet, like Edgar Chance, who could
foretell to a few minutes the time and also the place when
and where a cuckoo would lay, Andy could foretell the
moods of wind and waves. 'I reckon another thirty hours
of this punching,' he would say, 'then we'll have a hundred
miles of calm. And after that we'll have a fair wind.'
And it would turn out as he said. Meanwhile, if a squall
hit us from nowhere, that was merely local. A little
swearing and a slight adjustment of the wheel and all
would be well.

And that afternoon Andy was ashore with the certain
sure opinion that the reef would turn nasty soon again.
He had come ashore, as he was anxious to get every one
on board as quickly as possible. In another half-hour the
so-and-so reef would be so-and-so impossible.

Two days to Penrhyn. No reef trouble there: a channel
connects sea and sheltered water. Yet it isn't all plain
sailing; when we entered the lagoon there was a strong and
favouring wind, otherwise we might not have got through.
In that narrow pass there is only forty minutes of slack
water between rushing tides, and we were not there during
those forty minutes. The pilot had decided that the engine
could take us in against the current, but the pilot had not
been in touch with that machine for quite a long time.

Our speed became slower and slower. There were a few long moments when we seemed to make no progress whatever against the swirling water; then very gradually we gained the mastery.

All the inhabitants of the village had assembled to greet us. Boys were playing guitars, girls were singing. As we drew in to the wharf a sailing canoe rushed under our bows, like a terrier between one's legs. A cutter with sails well filled, on its way to the diving grounds, had already given us a welcome. All nine occupants of the boat had broken into dance, on the thwarts, on the gunwales, anywhere; some playing imaginary guitars, others performing a varied assortment of acrobatics.

The first thing we had seen on entering the lagoon was the *Taipi*, and the first person we met when we landed was her skipper, Captain Cambridge. 'Why, dammit, we thought you were really gone this time,' was the general greeting. It had taken us seven sailing days from Aitutaki. The *Taipi*, on a shorter course, had not been heard of for a month. Naturally, the worst had been assumed.

'People have got into the habit of thinking I 'm lost,' said Captain Cambridge. 'This is the twenty-second time they 've had the idea. I can't understand them. We got here in nice time for Christmas. That was all we expected to do. It 's true we had a spot of rough weather to start with,' he continued, 'but what she took on board wouldn't drown a cockroach. Then after the storm we had a week or two of calm; all we wanted was a bottleful of wind. I reckon the *Taipi* the best weather ship in the islands.'

To me she was more like an illustration in an early missal than anything in real life; and, somehow, looking at her commander, I got the impression of a medieval mystic. A quiet, gentle man with a kindly expression in his eyes, I would sooner have expected to meet him, peering at me through his glasses from behind the musty volumes of a second-hand bookshop than from behind the wheel of a schooner trading in those tough latitudes.

'Yes, he 's a good man, Captain Cambridge,' said a member of his crew. 'Doesn't drink, mind you, but he 's a good man for all that. Always the old pipe—and *tea!* Tea every fifteen minutes, and without sugar—without any sugar at all. He has a little Primus, and he makes his own tea—every fifteen minutes.'

'I 've got two vices,' said Captain Cambridge to me. 'Knitting socks for myself and chopping firewood for my wife. When I 'm at home I never give orders. All I ever say is: "Yes, Maggie." We get on well together, me and the wife.'

When I asked how long he was staying he said that he was in no hurry to get away. 'I like to get the new moon over before I meet the sun,' he said. He explained that at that time of year the sun was directly overhead in the latitude of Aitutaki, and that hurricanes are said to form directly under the sun. The weather is supposed to change at the time of the new moon, so he felt that the combination of the two was to be avoided.

'What 's a couple of weeks, anyway?' he said. 'I like to do my worrying ashore, then I can be quiet and peaceful when I 'm at sea. But it 's a queer thing,' he added, 'when I 'm at sea, if any gear is going to carry away, maybe a block come down or something like that, I can sense there 's something wrong before it happens. I get a kind of uneasy feeling. It's the same if anything's wrong at home. I can smell it, like the Maoris do.'

That evening Tangaloa, the mate of our schooner and a Penrhyn man, gave a party to celebrate our arrival. All the crew and all the passengers were there, and it seemed as if every islander was there also. Feasting and dancing were the order of the evening, and there was no lack of enthusiasm for either. But I spent most of the time talking to Tangaloa junior, His Majesty's wireless operator on the island. He told me of the 'invasion' in 1943.

'One day I sit talking to the priest in his house when there's a great knock-knock on the door. So we open the door and there's a man standing outside and he's shouting and calling out: "A plane, a plane—we seen a plane coming." So I look and I see nothing, but I start to run, and I run all the way to the radio station. And the priest —you know him, big fat man—he come running down the road, black coat all unbutton down the front. And I see policeman come running with his gun, waving it in the air, all ready to shoot that plane, only he forget ammunition at home. Everywhere people running, every one scared. Me scared, too. Some hide in the pandanus-trees, they get all cut and scratched, but they not care; they hide and they pray. And some hide in palm-trees, think maybe Jap not find them there. And some go into the church and pray. And fellow who keep store run out and leave door wide open, but no one steal that day, every one too frighten on account of that plane. And all the time I not see any plane. But I get to radio station, and I grab all papers and codes and I stick them inside my shirt, and then I try get Rarotonga but my hands keep jumping about; I can't hold them still. I think I turn on switch but nothing happen, so I think maybe valve burnt out. I look again at switch and it turned *off*, not on, so then I turn it on very careful, and I get Rarotonga and I tell them we got a plane. And they say: "You seen it? What kind of a plane?" And I say I not seen it, other men seen it, and they say: "You go and look at it, look at the mark." But I not like to leave radio, I tell 'nother man go look, and he come back very quick and he say he seen mark—*red zero*! So I tell Rarotonga, and they say: "You seen that yourself, that red zero?" And I say: "No, other man see it and he come tell me." So they say: "You go yourself and look at that mark." And then 'nother man come and he say big battleship out at sea, and 'nother man come and he say four boats coming full of soldiers. I tell them this over radio to Rarotonga, and they say: "Never mind that battleship, never mind those boats, what about mark on that plane?" So then I leave radio, and I run out and look myself. And I see plane out in lagoon, and I look at it and gee! I see a great white star! So I run back to the radio and I call out and I say: "It 's friendly plane; I seen big white star!"—I think when other man look, he only see little red zero in the middle of star. And the boys out diving mighty scared too. When they see plane coming, down they go to bottom, wait for bomb to drop. No bomb, up they come. Zoom, zoom, plane coming back—down they go again. Wait long time below. Up they come. Then one man see mark—big star, friendly plane, all laugh like hell.'

Our conversation turned to pearl fishing. Tangaloa told me that if when down below a diver sees a shark, he can signal to the other men near him by a kind of mooing grunt, which can be heard under the water. He told me, too, that the fishermen eat no food before going diving, at most a cup of tea or coffee in the early morning; but in the evening when they get back, after they have rested a while, they eat a hearty meal. In each group of divers a senior man will pray aloud for their safety before diving begins. Similarly, on their return, a prayer of thanksgiving is said before they leave their boats. 'But sharks only hurt you if you done wrong,' said Tangaloa. 'If a man go to court, and court let him off, but all the time he guilty, then next time when he go pearl diving the shark get him. One time here, time of New Year and every one practising hymns, one man thought he go out dive for shell. One of the deacons say: "You better not go, you stay and sing hymns." This man turn round and he say: "Will sing hymns give me food?" So the deacon say: "All right, if you want to go, you go." So he go out, and after 'bout one hour the boat come back with the black flag. And everybody say when they see boat coming back, they know what happen, 'cause when they put up black flag that mean someone hurt. If a man drown when diving they haul up black flag.'

Next day there wasn't a breath of wind, the lagoon was serene as the sky above it. Far out I could see the canoes of pearl divers. I had no difficulty in persuading the owner of a small launch to take me to the fishing-ground.

As we came near to the scene of action we could see pairs of dark heads above the water, each separated from

the other by about a yard. But a closer view showed that one of each pair of heads was in reality the end of a baulk of wood. When a diver goes to the fishing-grounds he takes with him in his canoe a log about five feet long, to one end of which a palm-leaf basket is attached. The basket is for the shell that he brings up, the other end of the log forms a kind of hobby horse on which he can sit while resting.

Around us now were several logs floating untended while their owners were below. On others divers were astride. All the men wore goggles either over their eyes or pushed up on their foreheads, and with their hair plastered down on their heads looked like strange creatures, half human, half marine. There was little talk between them, but an incessant whistling exhalation as they breathed long and deeply, with an occasional cry from one of them: 'E-e-e-ah!'

And, while we watched, a diver would slip from his log and, after swimming a few strokes with his face below the surface, would double up his body and shoot straight downwards—the last to be seen of him would be the soles of his feet showing pale yellow through the water. Other divers appeared at the surface, rising vertically, sometimes with one shell in their hands, sometimes with two. They

dropped these into their baskets and climbed on to their logs, balancing themselves there with fin-like movements of their hands. It was a quiet, matter-of-fact performance. Hereabouts the water is eleven fathoms. The divers do not stay below more than about a minute and a half.

Soon after we arrived at the scene, Mamalua, the pilot who had brought the *Tiare* through the pass the day before, came to the surface. Recognizing me, he swam towards the launch and handed me the shell he had just brought up.

'Pearl for you,' he panted, smiling. Others who heard him smiled too, because the chances against finding a pearl of any sort are reckoned as a thousand to one. But when I opened the shell there was a pearl inside; not a big one, but excellent in colour.

Captain Cambridge was standing on the shore when I got back.

'You were talking about octopus fishing last night,' he said, 'and you were saying that from Tonga to Tahiti there is the same story of the quarrel with the rat. Did you know that on Manihiki and Rakahanga, and on Takume in the Tuamotus, you will find the octopus coming on shore at night and catching the rats at the water's edge? What's more, it will sometimes come out on to the beach and lie there same as if it was dead, waiting for the rats to come along. You don't believe me? Well, it's true. I've seen it myself and so have plenty of others. And there's another thing which I haven't seen but which I've heard of, and that is that those same octopuses will climb a pandanus-tree that's near the water, to get the fruit. You'll see 'em in the morning hanging in the branches, but the moment they see you—plop, like a stone, they drop into the sea and are gone.

'"Sounds tall!" you say, and that's what I said, too. Then one day I came on a book by that missionary chap, Gill, and he says the very same thing.'

Captain Cambridge refilled his pipe and lit it.

'Yes,' he mused, 'once we've had that change of moon and the northerly's come in, I'm off. I don't like it ashore. I'm never well. Sea and sky, that's what I want, just sea and sky. It's never monotonous. It's always changing. The waves are changing and the clouds are changing and the shadows on the clouds are changing and the shadows of the clouds on the water are changing. It's never the same for two minutes. And at sunset and dawn the long rays of light fanning out from west to east and from east to west, over our heads, and meeting the opposite horizon, all curved like the lines of longitude. That's when I'm well—when I can't see as much sand as would stop a watch.'

CHAPTER THIRTY

MATARA, AN ELDERLY WOMAN, and Taruia, her brother, were twins. Neither could tell a story without the other. If I was talking to Matara and I asked her any particular question, she would go and call her brother. If I asked Taruia about a legend he would slip away and fetch his sister. For either of them to tell a story without the other was as impossible as for one pianist to play a duet. Together they would sit cross-legged on the ground, fixing me with their dark eyes. Then after a few whispers to each other the brother would open the recital; quietly at first, with the sister's voice a gentle echo of his own. Then, as the story proceeded the pace would grow faster; the voices now alternating, now synchronizing in perfect harmony. With identical gestures they emphasized their points. A resounding phrase in the bass would be triumphantly repeated in the treble. Simultaneously, as the drama reached its climax, they would leap to their feet, with eyes flashing and arms gesticulating as they re-enacted the scene they described, voices rising in dramatic crescendo. As they uttered the closing phrases the two would stand for a moment, wild-eyed and defiant, glaring at the listeners. Then their faces would relax into their usual gentle expressions, and they would look around, smiling deprecatingly, and resume their retiring positions on the floor.

It was from them that I heard the story of the strange *marae* a couple of miles from the village where I was staying. It is a platform of stones about four feet high, built with the outline of a headless figure, and is known as Te Papa-o-Sokoau, meaning 'the Refuge of Sokoau.'

'This girl Sokoau was from this village, and she was wife of a man whose name was Tonu, and they live on his island on other side of lagoon. And Tonu very fond of his wife because she most beautiful woman of all the islands. And one day Sokoau come to this village to stay with her father, and while she stay with her father she get playing around. So when she go back to Tonu, he have a slight know what she been doing, and he ask her and she say, "Yes, it is true." So, when she say that, he very mad. Whang! He hit on her head, and she die. Then the ghost of this girl go crying around and it come along tell her father, and then her father put up that grave. But Sokoau's body not there because Tonu cut it all up.'

There are the remains of more than twenty other *maraes* on Penrhyn, in many cases very slight remains thanks to the white man, but this one is unique; all the others, with one exception which is a close approximation, being of the standard pattern—a rectangular space enclosed by a low kerb of coral with tall upright slabs at intervals, and at one end a raised platform of stone. The general function of these *maraes*, which averaged about thirty yards in length and rather less in width, was both religious and secular. At times the ceremony might be entirely devout, at other times it might pertain more to conviviality, though even then, as with many of our own feasts, it would have a religious significance. It is said that the Papa-o-Sokoau became a refuge to which any one in danger of his life could fly and obtain immunity from attack as long as he remained within its precincts.

Matara and Taruia told me, too, of a chief who, 'before the Christian time,' lived on one of the northern islets. 'He would stand on the shore and wave with his hand, and the fish would come up on to the reef. If other chiefs came to him and said: "Our people hungry, they are starving for the fish," then he would stand up and tell the fish to come in. It was because the *mana* was given to him by the old gods that he was able to do this, and when he died he gave the *mana* to his children and they were able to do same thing. Sometimes when that chief stayed inside his house and the people came along, say they want fish, then he grab his stick and he point with that stick right through the sides of his house, and he wave, and when he wave the fish come up into the shallow water. Then the people go and take the fish, and when he think they got all they want he look around and he call out, "You got enough?" and everybody say: "Yes." Then he say: "Now all you fish still alive, you go back." And some would be dead—maybe some of the people step on them and they die—but all those ones still alive they turn round and they go back in sea again.'

And there was Tavake, a 'doctor' who had lived in our village. When a ship, the *Chatham*, was wrecked the men came ashore 'and they were all sick and nobody know how to fix them, so they were brought into this village to Tavake. When they were brought they were all unconscious. But Tavake run around and grab their spirits and put them back into their bodies, and everybody become conscious. That was the job of the doctors in old days, to put the spirits back.

'There was another doctor, called Saungaki, over at Hakasusa on the south side of the lagoon, and there was an evil spirit, a woman, who make love to him, and she pay him with the souls of the people who die. When a man die here, this woman take the soul to Hakasusa and give it to the doctor. Then the relations must go there from this village, and they take with them for the doctor plenty good food, and then the doctor he say, "Yes," and he come back with the relations in canoe, and he bring soul back with him, and he put it into dead person, and that person live again.'

The *Chatham* to which the twins referred was wrecked on Penrhyn in 1853, and the only record that we have of life on the island before the advent of Christianity comes from E. H. Lamont, one of the owners of the ship, who subsequently spent a year on the atoll. His welcome was no less vociferous than ours had been, if not quite so reassuring. He writes: 'A shout from the bows informed us that the natives were coming on us; and on looking over the side we saw them advancing with spears and clubs, which they brandished, uttering at the same time the most frightful yells, accompanied by horrid grimaces and contortions.'

However, after a parley between a native of Aitutaki who was on board the ship and some natives on the reef, the immediate prospect seemed less grim, and that evening Lamont found himself the guest of a family who lived in 'a little hamlet' a short distance from the site of the wreck. It was 'in an open space, strewed with white gravel from the sea beach, and planted round with young coco-nut trees, whose bright leaves completely shaded the three little huts that half occupied the space; while another, partially hidden by some pandanus-trees, was evidently the cook-house. The white gravelled plot was scrupulously clean, and looked prettily bright in the surrounding darkness of the forest.' As he sat on the mat that had been spread for him he was surprised to find that 'they did not seem the same yelling savages I had beheld all day. They had now the appearance of rational beings, spoke quietly, and I even thought kindly to each other, and frequently laughed with a pleasant cheerfulness that astonished me.'

Even so he was not entirely reassured and he slept little that night, for between the hardness of his bed and pillow, anxiety for the future, and the excitement of the day past, his mind was 'ill disposed for rest.'

Next day his worst forebodings seemed likely to be fulfilled when, with all the members of the crew, he was marched under guard to a *marae* about a mile from the village. It was 'a rugged and bleak spot,' he says. 'Blocks of coral rock were strewed around and piled in masses of every form, as if rent and upheaved by an earthquake. The tall *fara* weed grew rank, showing that the spot was rarely visited. Numerous pandanus-trees darkened more than usual the deep shade of the grove, but not enough to hide the tall stones of a 'mara' (or sacred ground) that appeared beyond. There were few or none of our party who were not aware that, on the Marquesas and other islands where cannibalism is practised, such spots were dedicated to these horrible orgies—their fellow beings being here offered as a sacrifice to their gods. The women and children, who are not allowed to enter these holy precincts, now stopped with looks of fear, whilst all the men proceeded a few paces further.'

Then began a most alarming ceremony. Young men rushed about waving spears 'with the most horrid contortions of visage.' The high priest, seated on the altar, 'began to glance wildly round in every direction. . . . A trembling motion, commencing in his hands, extended through his whole body till every limb shook in the most violent manner, the muscles working and the veins swelling almost to bursting.'

By this time Lamont, the doctor who was part-owner with him of the ship, and the captain, all of whom had been singled out for special attention, were convinced that there was only one possible conclusion to the ceremony. When each of the three was given a coco-nut which had already been used in the ceremonial and told to eat it, their fears seemed confirmed. 'I think we may bid farewell to each other, Lamont,' said the doctor.

But there was still further ritual to be observed before the end. The natives having led their captives to a little pool of fresh water, plunged into it 'and, stooping their heads, with a peculiar action of the arms splashed themselves over as ducks do with their wings,' urging the white men to do likewise. When that was over the party was marched to a clear space near the beach, where the women performed what Lamont considered 'a very absurd dance.' But he was probably not in any great humour to enjoy the finer shades of rhythm.

After the dance, as if to disperse any last ray of hope that might have remained in the captives' breasts, the assembled crowd began a wailing, at first plaintive, then rising to piercing and unearthly yells, the women shaking their heads and weeping as they looked at the white men, men and women alike lacerating themselves with shells. 'Before they ceased their legs, arms, and faces were streaming with blood, and as they wiped the ever-flowing tears, now mingling with the red stream on their cheeks, their visages became perfectly horrific.'

And then, for the last act of the drama, the company was marched back to where they had started from in the morning, and there—the 'victims' were set free. Had they but known it the whole ceremony constituted their formal reception into the community, removing any *tapu* that they might have brought with them from other lands, and bringing them into spiritual accord with the people of the island. The young men rushing about the *marae* with spears were driving away any evil spirits that might have been hovering in the vicinity; the agitation of the priest showed that he had been possessed by a god; the three coco-nuts were given to those who appeared to be of the highest rank, as recognition of their status. The ablutions in the pool were to remove the *tapu* of the *marae*, and permit those who had participated in the sacred ceremony to mix again with their fellows. The dancing was in the traditional form that celebrated the meeting of different communities, the wailing and mutilation expressed grief for those who had recently died; a stranger could not become one of the community if he did not share in its past sorrows. To-day among the Maoris of New Zealand there is a similar wailing when a kinsman returns to his family.

From that time forth each of the white men was the chosen child of some leading man in the place, standing in the same position to all his relations as his own children, and even enjoying some additional privileges. Any lack of welcome in the first place had only been in accordance with custom, there being so much inter-islet raiding of coconut plantations at that time that, before visitors were allowed to land, they had to explain the purpose of their visit.

This raiding, with consequent reprisals, was a constant source of war, and the power and prestige of individual islets, often dependent on alliances made or broken, varied continually. But in the hostilities a pretty etiquette was observed. Before a general engagement it was not uncommon for the opposing forces to sit down at a short distance from each other and discuss matters. Then, if the invaders could give no just cause for their arrival, the fight would begin with showers of stones and spears. Women were always in the forefront of the battle, endeavouring with light clubs to break the spears of the opposing party—it being a point of honour that they would be unharmed by the men. After the supply of stones and spears had been exhausted the men fought at closer quarters with clubs—the women stepping aside to have a private fight of their own with fists. So highly was a tuft of hair from the head of an enemy regarded that before an engagement women would cut short the greater part of their own hair, lest any of it should become a trophy of their opponents.

The dress of the men at this time was the *maro*, a narrow band of leaves that passed between the legs and encircled the waist. The women wore the *titi*, a short kilt of coconut leaves slit into fine strips like grass, cut square above the knee.

Lamont spent twelve months on Penrhyn, and had plenty of time to visit the many islets along its forty-mile perimeter. I was there for only twelve days. But one morning a launch was going to collect copra from Mangarongaro, the islet on which the *Chatham* was wrecked, about six miles from the village of Omoka, where I was staying. Why not go in it? I was asked. Why not indeed? And why not a dozen others also? We'd have a picnic!

It took some time for the party to collect on the launch. Most of them were from the *Tiare*—half a dozen of the crew, six or eight passengers, and a couple of small children. The awning was rigged over the after-deck of the launch and the women gathered there; the men preferred to sit in the sun, for'ard. Fishing-lines were produced; a couple of long barbed spears and two guns were stowed away. A guitar was fetched from the schooner.

There was a slight head wind, but the lagoon was scarcely ruffled when we set out. The helmsman, standing in the stern, played the guitar as, with the tiller between his shins, he steered a course among the coral heads. We reached Mangarongaro, but it seemed a pity not to go further— the copra could be picked up on our return journey. So we continued another few miles to a group of small islets where innumerable birds were wheeling overhead. Anchoring at the edge of the fringing reef, we waded some quarter of a mile to the shore through ankle-deep water. Here a small sand shark swam lazily, its pale-cream body hardly visible against the sunlit coral; there a sea-eel, coiled in a crevice, glared at us with open-mouthed malevolence. The water was hot to our feet, the narrow beach was dazzlingly white, but there was cool green shade under the palms. Quickly two men climbed trees and threw down nuts; as quickly the nuts were husked and opened for drinking. Except for two women who stayed to make a fire, every one scattered in search of food. Women went on to the reef to collect shell-fish, men went there with spears for fish. Two men with the guns went into the bush.

Shots were soon heard, and a little later the small boys of the party appeared carrying the great limp bodies of half a dozen frigate birds. Then the fishermen returned with an abundance of rainbow-coloured parrot-fish slung on their spears. Women brought crayfish and sea-urchins. The birds were soon prepared and put to cook in the oven, with fish, breadfruit and taro, among the hot stones, while the meat from the sea-urchins was treated with the juice of fresh limes. A young palm had been cut down and the growing tip was chopped for salad—crisp and white as celery.

Along the tide-marks of the lagoon, and for some distance above it, lay the usual jumble of coco-nut husks, decaying fronds, dead flower spikes from the palms, and much other litter. Land-crabs of varying colours were scavenging in the debris. While we waited for the opening of the oven, I noticed a large green crab with crimson claws feeding from the fallen spathe of a coco-nut flower. It was sidling along, dipping first one claw and then the other into the boat-like trough, and carrying fragments of food from it to its mouth—the movements of its ungainly claws as delicate as those of the daintiest fingers.

Pepe, the helmsman of the launch, interrupted my thoughts. 'Where you come from?' he asked. 'New Zealand?'

'Ireland,' I told him.

'Oh, you Irish,' he said, and forthwith began to sing *Killarney*.

'You know that song?' he asked at the end of the first verse.

'I do,' I said, 'and I know Killarney, too.'

'The sister at the school at Rarotonga, she teach us that. We call her Sister Killarney because she say Killarney much better than Raro. She say Killarney mountains and Killarney lagoons much more good-looking than Raro. What you think?'

I said: 'Killarney is the most beautiful place in all the world.'

'That what Sister say, too. But Father David, he say France best place. He and Sister they often have big fights and big laughs 'bout that. And Father Melville he say they both wrong, he say no place like New York. I think no place like Raro, but I Rarotonga boy; maybe that why I think that.'

CHAPTER THIRTY-ONE

THE *TAIPI* BEAT US to the channel, but once outside the reef we soon parted company. She was heading south for Rarotonga, and our nose was pointed south-east for Tahiti. The 'northerlies' for which we had been waiting at Penrhyn had set in. It might have been the beginning of a yacht race the way the two ships crossed the starting line, and as far as the *Tiare* was concerned it might have been a yacht's cruise all the way to Tahiti, with a fair wind, and an occasional shower to cool the deck and give us all a bath. On schooners there are no great facilities for ablutions, but it 's a poor squall that provides no one with a wash. Under the boom of the mainsail is the best place for a shower, though some prefer the spout from the roof of the deck-house. Others, again, like to block up the scuppers with a few old clothes and sit in comfort in the lake that soon forms. I could tell a pretty story of a lady of the lake and a flash of lightning on a dark night, half-way between Penrhyn and Tahiti, but owing to the rain I missed a drawing and 'twould be only half the story without the illustration.

On the morning of the fifth day out from Penrhyn, as the first faint light of dawn crept into the sky, a heavy cloud low on the horizon resolved itself into the rugged triangular mass of Borabora. From the east that island has perhaps the most striking silhouette of any island in the Pacific, appearing as a huge pyramid rising directly out of the sea, but from the north, as we were then approaching, its outline, with the long western flank visible, resembled a gigantic lion *couchant*.

The sky was in keeping with the grandeur of the land. Heavy turbulent clouds passed in stately procession. Lightning flashed and thunder echoed. Once it seemed as if a burst of flame leapt from the sea to meet the firmament above. With the growing light the smoke-grey clouds were streaked and splashed with the warmer tints of dawn, and then far to the south-east we could see Tahaa, shielding from our sight Raiatea, the holy island, the island from which after its first settlement, about the fifth century A.D., all Polynesian cultures spread. At sunset that day we passed Huahine, dark peaks against a lemon sky; and then, next morning, through a golden smother of mist, we saw the peaks and pinnacles of Moorea pricking their pall of clouds. Out of the same mist, scarcely distinguishable from its sister isle, there lay ahead of us Tahiti, our final landfall.

Soon after I left Tahiti in 1929 I received a letter from James Norman Hall, with whom I had stayed. He wrote: 'We have pulled down the old native house in which you lived and are building a bigger one instead. It is yours whenever you wish, for as long as you wish. We call it "The House that waits for Robert."' When, eighteen years later, I landed again in Tahiti I found a letter which said: '"The House that waited" is still waiting: use it and everything that is in it as your own, and use my other house across the road in any way that you please.' Hall was in America and couldn't get back to Tahiti before I left.

When you have scarcely seen a book for eighteen months it is pleasant to find yourself in a library. When you have heard no music but that of drums and guitars for eighteen months it is stimulating to find yourself with a first-class gramophone and a collection of classical records. The walls of my house were lined with books: Oxford Companions, Cambridge Histories; chronicles of nations, of navies, of exploration. Hundreds of volumes of poetry, scores of volumes of plays. Philosophies, biographies, memoirs, and diaries. And, near by, albums of records: trios, quartets, symphonies, 'and all kinds of music.' In Polynesia, where life is tranquil, there is only the twanging of the guitar; but in the turmoil and agony of other civilizations exquisite music is brought into being.

Outside my house there is a murmuring of waters; a two-way tide of pencilled foam greeting a mountain stream —the trio of the reef. In the cities the blurred sounds from without a concert hall are a distraction to the listener, but the music of the reef is an augmentation of the orchestra. I listen to Chopin—liquid notes of rivulets; I listen to Mozart—bird song of flute beside the tumbling waters of the harp. In front of where I live the reef is broken, but there is no harbour. The lagoon is shallow and filled with intersecting ramparts of dead coral, which break the force of the ocean waves before they reach the land. The foreshore is of grey volcanic sand. Myna birds chatter as they pick among the debris at the water line. Flocks of small finches, blazed with crimson, feed among the grasses. An upturned canoe, deep blue in colour, lies beneath a *fau* bush, whose yellow blossoms scattered on the ground have turned to bronze; another canoe, its red timber still unfinished, lies beside the stump of the tree from which it has been carved. A young man leads a horse into the lagoon and throws water over it with an empty coco-nut shell. In the shallows four dogs are

playing; slim and shining like mantelpiece dogs of glass, they leap from rock to rock and splash through the pools, chasing an elusive heron. Far out on the reef a woman with a bamboo rod is fishing; and beyond, in the open sea, a schooner is heading for the Tuamotus.

And when I grow tired of looking seawards I have Madame de Sévigné, Cervantes, de Quincey, Max Beerbohm, and many others for company. Not that I am 'a great reader.' On the contrary, like Montaigne, I rarely read 'except at those hours when the tedium of doing nothing drives me to it.' Then I like sufficient of a book to stimulate my thoughts, not enough of it to jade my mind. Long hours of study do not suit my temperament. I am far from being one of those who, as Seneca says, 'carry intemperance into the study of literature.' I am more in sympathy with Emerson's idea that 'the rich mind lies in the sun and sleeps.'

All in all, I agree with Hazlitt that 'the indefatigable readers of books are like the everlasting copiers of pictures, who, when they attempt to do anything of their own, find they want an eye quick enough, a hand steady enough, and colours bright enough, to trace the living forms of nature.'

But enough of books. It is pleasant to lounge on the waterfront in Papeete and watch the schooners and phosphate ships and launches and fishing canoes come and go. As Ogden Nash wrote:

'It is pleasant to gaze at the sailors,
To gaze without having to sail.'

A line of schooners is leashed to the *quai*, sprit beyond sprit pointing to the open sea. One looks through a maze of rigging, new spars and old spars, freshly painted stays and rusty stays, to the pink-flowered acacia-trees that shade the waterfront. There is the *Denise* that was wrecked in the Austral Isles and lay on the reef for several months before she could be refloated. The *Vaite* went on the reef at Raroia in the Tuamotus, and the *Vahine* did likewise at Haraiki in the same group. There is a yacht-like ship whose extra speed helped to quench the thirst of many an American during prohibition times.

Most of the schooners are sheltering till the hurricane season is over. Their sails have been stowed, and the crew relax under the awnings. Those ships that have recently arrived look dingy and bedraggled after months at sea. Others float proudly as sea birds in the glory of new plumage, white hulls reflecting emerald and hyacinth, copper shining at the water's edge. The hulls rise and fall gently, their reflections dance in the shimmering water, *Les Sylphides* of the sea. The wake of a passing launch billows behind it like the frou-frou of a dancer's skirts. Everything is more like ballet than real life. Instead of *La Boutique fantasque* it is *Le Quai fantasque*. A man in a crimson shirt and dark-blue trousers capers to the water trough on the pier. He takes off his wide-brimmed straw hat, fills it with water and replaces it on his head, letting the water run down over his body. Hatful after hatful he pours in this way. Then, taking off his shirt and using the hat as a basin, he washes his neck and shoulders. While he is thus occupied a gramophone in a nearby café begins to play the 'Toreador' song from *Carmen*. Immediately the washing is performed in time to the music. Finally, after drinking at the tap, the actor replaces his hat on his head and dances off, waving his shirt as if at an imaginary bull. He has hardly left the stage when a young man in tight-fitting olive-green trousers and a lemon-coloured shirt rides past on a pale blue bicycle, playing a ukulele as he goes, his hands far from the handlebars.

And as I stand watching, I am accosted by an old friend who, since our last meeting, has done a long sentence for barratry. 'You haven't even got a grey hair,' I say. 'It's a wig,' he replies, raising it a moment as one might a hat.

Among timber houses, flimsy as a painted backcloth, the actors come and go. There is a continuous procession of colour, both literal and metaphorical, a mixture of French and Chinese cultures superimposed on the Tahitian. Little of the pure Polynesian remains in Tahiti to-day; the native has been absorbed. As I watch, a Chinese coolie trots past with a carrying-pole and basket. Another Chinaman stands at a corner of the street selling oranges and slices of water-melon. A crimson water-cart passes, spraying the street. A dark-skinned girl with ebony hair to her hips trips by in crocus-yellow shorts and sun-top; another in plum-coloured slacks and white shirt stands under a brick-red poster. There is a *chic* here not known in the other islands. The Samoans have too much natural dignity to need it; they wear their clothes with unconscious pride, the Tahitians wear them with conscious provocation.

And the whole scene can change as quickly as on a stage. I was sitting at a café on the waterfront when of a sudden the sunlight was blotted out. Rain began to fall. Colour gave way to monotone. Moorea, usually so clear across the water, disappeared. Even the surf on the reef, scarcely a quarter of a mile away, was soon lost to sight. The rain became a deluge. A phosphate ship of nine thousand tons, whose bulk had dwarfed everything else in the harbour, looked like a child's water-colour blot on paper. There was no wind: an umbrella would have kept the largest waist-line dry. Soon the drainings of the streets had so discoloured the water that lagoon and waterfront were hardly distinguishable one from the other. Then the rain ceased, and without warning a great wind struck the harbour. The water became rough: crisp, angry waves, as in a Dutch seascape, broke over the pier and quayside. Schooners and yachts tugged at their moorings. Twigs and branches of the trees showered on to the street; the ground was soon strewn with green boughs and flowers as if in the wake of some procession. Empty barrels rolled along the wharf and were blown into the sea. Small boats went adrift and were carried across the bay.

Ships were plucking at their anchors, many were already dragging them. A cutter was broadside on to the wharf, battered by every wave. Sails were tearing loose and thrashing in the gale. Schooners with engines cut their moorings and stood out to sea. Those without engines could only trust to their hawsers, hawsers that were yielding under the strain.

As suddenly as the wind had arisen it fell. An hour after the first onslaught the waters of the harbour were calm again. Only the mountains showed change: their forms, earlier shrouded in mist, now stood crisp and clear as in an oil painting newly varnished.

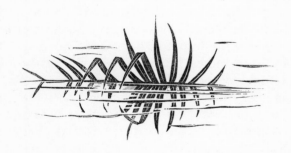

CHAPTER THIRTY-TWO

RARELY IN TAHITI does one eat or drink alone. There is always someone who invites you to a table. In a bar it may be a group of old-timers who, sitting in their favourite corner, are spinning their endless variations of old-time yarns; or in a restaurant it may be philosophers who are reasoning about the unreasonable.

At the Diadème I heard of Captain John Dow, an American who, a year or two after he had retired from the sea, lost all his savings in some financial crash. Wandering one day by a boat-yard, he saw the hull of an old yacht thrown on one side. 'Only fit for firewood,' he was told. 'Give her to me,' he said, 'and I'll take her off your hands.' So they gave him the hulk, and he and a companion set to and repaired it, and eventually they sailed together from New York for the West Indies. The companion died on the way, and Dow was afraid to heave the body overboard for fear he'd be accused of murder. So he had to carry it in the boat with him for days until he reached land. From the West Indies he continued alone, through the Panama Canal, to the Galapagos, and from there to the Marquesas and then on to Manihiki. By the time he reached there his boat was in a bad way, leaking at every seam. But he carried on and managed to make Pangopango, in American Samoa. There he met a senior naval officer who had once been a shipmate of his, and that officer gave the yacht such an overhaul that her owner hardly recognized it. Dow was next heard of in the Tokelaus, and after that nothing more was known of him until his yacht was found hove-to in mid-ocean with the flag at half-mast and he dead in his bunk.

There was a story of a native who had found a large pearl and taken it to a Chinese trader. The Chinaman, having examined the pearl, said: 'Looks like me getting out and you getting in.' They put the pearl in the resident agent's safe for the night, and the next day the Chinaman handed over the store, lock, stock, and barrel, and took the pearl in exchange.

There was the story, too, of Jackie, the bos'n of one of the schooners, who, as a young man, had eloped with a girl from Penrhyn. They were over thirty days at sea in a canoe before they reached Samoa, by which time they were so sick of looking at each other that the first thing the girl did on getting ashore was to marry someone else.

One evening at Thirel's bar I was joined by Andy, who had just come back from a visit to the far side of the island. 'The Irish—what delightful people to meet!' he said. 'They're not idle, it's just that they don't do anything. They don't *need* to do anything, they do it all by imagining. To hear them talk you'd think you were travelling all over the world with a million bucks in your pocket, and all the time you're just sitting on a bench. Now there's that fellow Murphy. Many's the time I've sat with him on his veranda—three sheets of tin and one and a half posts—and he'll be talking of the improvements he has planned for his house—a library on the top floor, a dance hall down below with a gallery for a Hungarian band, and under the flamboyant tree a fountain with coloured lights and a pool for the girls to swim in. And when I go along next year, he'll still be sitting there on the old veranda with the sheets of tin more rusty than ever, and he'll be that busy with thinking and planning you'd hardly like to disturb him. He's as rich as any man in the world. He's got everything he wants—in imagination.'

Monsieur Laforce, a Swiss, came and sat at our table. For twenty years he had had a plantation in Tahiti, and till a few weeks earlier he had never thought to live elsewhere. Then one night in Papeete he saw a film of Switzerland. For three days after that he had gone about as if in a dream; for three nights he hadn't slept. The only things he could think of were those snow-covered mountains and the village where his sisters lived. Within a week he had sold all that belonged to him on the island, and now he was in town awaiting the first boat that would take him to Europe.

A local celebrity came and stood beside us. He swayed gently as he spoke. 'I am now on my way home,' he said. 'I may not get there. To-morrow I will be going to my office; I may not get there. That is the Islands.'

He moved to some friends at another table.

'I think that gentleman have three little sheets in the wind,' said Monsieur Laforce.

Upstairs great thoughts were being bandied across the dinner tables. One heard of 'that constant war between instinct and intelligence, in which the former desires immortality and the latter denies its possibility'; that 'marriage was created a sacrament by those who practise celibacy'; that 'opinions rarely become accepted before they are out of date.'

There has for many years been a small nucleus of intellectuals in Tahiti. A few live there permanently, the rest are passers-by. There are ethnologists, some of whom through a comparison of the string-figure games played throughout the islands find affinities of lineage, others who trace genealogies and histories through ancient songs and chants. There are geologists who study the formation of volcanic peaks, and zoologists who explore the coral reefs, and botanists who inquire into the food values of native plants. There was one man I knew who devoted years of his life to research on the mosquito that carries the filarial infection of elephantiasis. There are always one or two authors, always one or two artists; on my last visit there was a pianist who played superbly. It is these men that one will find, quietly contemplative amid the blare of gramophones. They represent the only culture to be found on the island. The Tahitian way of life is dead. The ancient customs have been forgotten.

Yet sometimes I wondered if strange powers were not active, resentful of the change. During the whole of my stay in Tahiti there was scarcely a night when I did not wake with a sense of horror, feeling a presence beside me that gripped at my arms or clutched at my throat. Three other visitors to whom I mentioned the subject had all suffered in a similar way. I am told it is the same in the Marquesas Islands, seven hundred miles to the north-east. It cannot have been just excess of *langouste*, or sufficiency of Musigny.

But much as I like congenial company at meals there are times when I prefer to eat, ostensibly, alone. Then I can hold converse with any of my friends, wherever they happen to be, in this world or the next. Friends who dine with me when I am alone never disagree; the meal is a feast of harmony. I spent a very pleasant evening on Mangaia when Charles Lamb came to dinner. I put before him a roast sucking pig, served whole as they do in the Islands, and afterwards I let him take his choice from the score or so of pineapples that were hanging on my veranda.

Then one night in Papeete I strayed with John Gay into a Chinaman's restaurant in a back street. It was after we had 'got over the impediment to a writer of water drinking' that he suggested 'Over the reefs and far away' as a possible title for this book.

CHAPTER THIRTY-THREE

THE CAPTAIN OF A SCHOONER was standing on the *quai* at the foot of his gangway. The crowd that had collected to see the schooner leave was wondering why her departure was delayed. She was bound for the Marquesas, with the usual mixed cargo—flour, beef, butter, salt, soap, roofing iron, cement, rope, oil, and a deck-load of passengers—and would return with copra, coffee, and oranges.

The mate was at the wheel. Passengers were leaning over the after-rail, calling repeated good-byes. Then a girl hurtled into the crowd on a bicycle, threw the machine against a bollard, rushed up to the captain, hung a wreath of flowers around his neck, kissed him on both cheeks, and mounting her bicycle again disappeared as quickly as she had come. After that the captain went on board, the gangway was hauled in, cables were cast off, and with the engine stuttering the schooner moved towards the reef.

No one kissed the captain or me or any one else that I could see when, a week later on another ship, the *Hiro*, I sailed for Anaa in the Tuamotus. Perhaps it was because the engineer was feeling thwarted that his engine ceased to *marche* before we had gone a mile from the shore. The vessel did not carry sails, and as we drifted slowly but unmistakably towards the breakers on the reef, a large black shark came and cruised around us. It gave me a lonely feeling. But soon the old hull began to quiver again and we headed once more for Anaa, two hundred and forty miles to the east.

Anaa is said to be the most productive atoll of that 'cloud' of seventy-six coral islands which, to the east of Tahiti, are spread across a thousand miles of ocean. Bougainville, when there in 1768, named them 'the Dangerous Archipelago,' and they still merit the name. Strong currents run between the islands, and there are numerous reefs, charted and uncharted. With one exception all the islands are atolls; scarcely any have land more than thirty feet above sea level, most of them do not reach half that height. Some have lagoons a hundred miles in circumference, others but a few miles in diameter.

Normally from a schooner's deck you cannot see an atoll at more than twelve miles, but you can steer your course to Anaa from fifty miles away by the bluish-green light that is reflected into the sky from its lagoon. The floor of that lagoon is of yellow sand and the waters are shallow, nowhere more than nine fathoms and in most places much less. From only one other atoll in the Tuamotus, Kaukura, is the same shade of colour reflected. It is told that Anaa came into being when a female deity by the name of Tekura-i-te-atua descended from the firmament of heaven and rested awhile in a cloud that hung low over the sea. Calling to her the seven spirits who control the seven currents of the ocean, she commanded that the seven currents should stir up the sand of the sea-floor so that it would form an island. And when that work was completed and the whole chain of islets had been raised above the sea Tekura took up permanent residence in the cloud, giving to it some of the blue colour of the firmament. When she unpins her hair and lets it blow in the wind one sees a change of colour in the cloud.

The supercargo of the *Hiro* said that he had a friend on Anaa who would probably fix me up with a bed. 'He spoke true.' On our arrival, Monsieur Aumerin took it as a matter of course that I should stay in his house. His family took it as a matter of course that they should vacate their double double-bedded bedroom and leave me with accommodation for four. Once again I got a feeling of loneliness. Monsieur Aumerin, of French extraction though for the most part speaking 'native,' knew enough French to understand as much French as I knew. We got along splendidly. The only thing that I regretted was the absence of Fred Wiseman from Tonga. He could have simplified his basic language still further. Monsieur Aumerin had that wonderful command of guttural expletives peculiar to the French. Other nations have basic sounds, but they are no nearer to the real bouquet than 'port type' is to port. Though born and bred on that out-of-the-way island, he had all a Frenchman's love of the things that really matter in life — claret, for instance, or a good omelette. And when on such subjects our agreement was unqualified he would lean back in his chair and give utterance to a resonant, appreciative 'Aw-w-w' that would roll upwards and outwards and fill the whole room where we were sitting. It did not matter the subject: he could strike the same chord in many keys.

Instead of the tangle of rotting palm fronds and rat-eaten coco-nuts which so often cover the surface of an atoll, there was orderliness and cultivation throughout this island. There were lawns of fine grass and carefully tended gardens in the village. The horses, with their small narrow heads, had a French elegance; even the dogs had the spry sophistication of the French bull-terrier. And as if to heighten that emerald enamel of the lagoon, many of the canoes had been painted delicate shades of carmine. The French have an appreciation of colour nuances that is lacking in Anglo-Saxon countries.

During my stay on Anaa every one was busy with the copra loading, but Monsieur Aumerin found time to take me across the lagoon to see other islets. When we landed on Puhuahara I thought that I had at last found the story-book coral island. The sandy beach shelved into crystal-clear water. Under the palms there was cool grass and a profusion of flowering shrubs. There were no mosquitoes, scarcely a fly. And a cooling breeze, always a cooling breeze, he said. While the two of us sat on the shore and dealt with garlic sausage and *vin rouge*, I thought to myself: 'Here is the place to live!'

Then I noticed that many of the palms had a curious change of direction midway in their growth. Whereas at first they leaned low over the ground or the lagoon, the stems of a sudden turned almost vertically upwards.

'C'est le cyclone,' said Monsieur Aumerin, with a shrug of his shoulders. All those palms that were so bent had been young trees in 1906. Then the hurricane came, and blew them nearly flat. After the storm they began to grow upwards again; the upright part of the trunk represented forty years of growth.

Though only a boy at the time, Monsieur Aumerin remembered the hurricane clearly. He had been living on the island with his parents. It was the worst *ouragan* they had ever had; a little one in 1903, but not very serious. In 1906 the sea had come right over the island. It was five feet deep in the village. Nothing could stand up against the waves. House after house was carried away. His parents had taken him to a part of the island where the trees and the bush broke the force of the waves, otherwise, like so many others, he would have been drowned. In the villages, with the open roads, there was nothing to stop the sea.

A few hundred yards from where we were sitting there was evidence of all this destruction. Former churches and other stone buildings were roofless shells. Foundation after foundation showed where large houses had once stood. Here and there rough native shelters had been built on these old foundations, but otherwise the village was desolate. Grass tracks marked where roads had been. We picked a few oranges from the sole remaining tree of a large plantation.

Other villages of the atoll had suffered even more. One, with all its inhabitants, had been completely wiped out. Before the hurricane there had been about fifteen hundred people on Anaa; to-day there are scarcely half that number.

The 'little one' in 1903, to which Monsieur Aumerin referred, had been far from little elsewhere. Takume and Raroia, each less than two hundred miles to the north-east, and Hikueru, about the same distance due east, and Marokau, a few miles south of Hikueru, had all suffered grievous disaster. On Marokau ninety-five people lost their lives, and on Hikueru three hundred and seventy-three.

The captain of the French ship *L'Excelsior*, who reached Hikueru on 22nd January, a week after the storm, wrote in his report: 'As soon as we were ashore the resident doctor met us and told us of the tragedy that had occurred. All the houses had been destroyed, the produce, the trading stores, the cutters, nearly four hundred people drowned or killed among the falling houses. The people who before the storm had been on that part of the island where we were then standing, and those who had managed to reach there after the storm began, were the only ones left alive. The scene before us was pitiable; everything to right and left was wrecked, the ground under the few coco-nut palms that remained, which had been a refuge for the eight hundred and ninety-six survivors, was a field of desolation. The trees, shorn of their fronds, had fallen in all directions, one on top of another. Natives and Europeans who were gathered here and there in groups were silent as if numbed.'

Two days later, from Marokau, the same officer records: 'I arrived on Marokau on the twenty-fourth of January at half-past five in the morning, opposite to where the village had once been, for it was now completely wiped out. No longer any houses, no longer any inhabitants, nothing remained. I went ashore with the chief engineer and we walked over the site of the village. All that remained of it was heaped in one small area about a hundred yards long, thirty yards wide, and four or five feet high. Everything was thrown together, remains of houses, bales of goods, boxes, fronds of trees, and, probably, under them corpses. On top of them all a wrecked launch. Everywhere broken palms, on all sides palms uprooted and thrown into the lagoon. Most of the broken trees had a cord attached to them with which some unfortunate being had tried to save himself from the sea. On two boards outside a temporary shelter we read the inscription: "Ninety-five are dead, eighty-five still alive have taken refuge on one of the islets to the south-east of the atoll."'

The commandant of another ship, the *Zélée*, having visited Raroia, wrote: 'This island has been destroyed, ravaged. It is unrecognizable. The destruction is comparable with that on Hikueru. Three-quarters of the coconut palms are broken and lying on the ground, mixed up with the wrecks of houses, of schooners, and of cutters, some of which have been thrown two hundred yards inland.' Similar reports came from other islands, in particular Napuka, Amanu, and Hao. It was only twenty-five years since a similar disaster had swept the group.

But, if one seeks for a few words to express the horror and the tragedy of these occurrences, nothing more simple or more eloquent could be found than the following brief mention in an official French handbook of L'Archipel des Tuamotu:

'Vienne un cyclone, la plage est balayée, le lagon déborde. Les cases et les cocotiers arrachés flottent à la dérive. Quant aux habitants, tant mieux pour eux s'ils peuvent fuir, dans leur minces pirogues, devant la tempête; sinon, ils sont engloutis.'

CHAPTER THIRTY-FOUR

'FOR SECURITY and the goodness of its bottom it is not inferior to any harbour I have met with in any of the islands. . . . The harbour has a romantic cast which renders it a prospect superior to anything in Tahiti.' So wrote Captain Cook, of Papetoai Bay in Moorea, and of the adjoining bay which now bears his name he thought no less highly. At last he and I were in agreement on landing

places. Here on all sides were subjects offering themselves, not only to the sympathetic brushes of oil and water-colour, but to that austere weapon of book decoration, the burin. Everything is crisp and clear-cut. Even the tenuous mist that creeps through secret aisles, revealing hidden spurs and coombs, or the vaporous clouds that tumble like waterfalls from a ledge, are all precise and definite in form. It is a valley of silhouettes, dark shapes on light, light shapes against dark, each with its own enriching patina.

The grandeur of the hills is the grandeur of gargantuan architecture. From the drowned amphitheatre rise pillars, buttresses, and broken arches; jagged outlines suggest fragments of a frieze. Everything is to scale; mosses and lichens have become giant ferns, swallows have changed to terns, and, instead of field-mice, land-crabs scuttle and scramble.

Ever changing, a wisp of cloud divides two peaks; a moment earlier they seemed but one, their outlines indistinct in haze. At one moment the mist hides the foot-hills, leaving the summits remote; at the next it annihilates all but the lowest shore. Even on nights when the moon is full the great crest of Rotui not only darkens the sky but, with its reflection, blackens the water at its feet.

The hotel in Cook's Bay stands on the shore of the lagoon. From the door of my bedroom it is but three paces to the water's edge; it is three more to ankle depth. Then the sand shelves sharply. It slides from under my feet and I float in deep water. Here in the coolness of early morning I watch the rising sun touch peak after peak. Here in the coolness of the evening I watch shadows creeping upwards. At night there is silence save for the lapping of the wavelets on the beach.

The sand is powdered with minute golden florets of the palms. On one tree the seven clusters of nuts show every stage of growth from the scarce-formed fruit, like acorns, to the full nuts about to fall. In the shallow water a cage of split bamboo for holding live bait is tied to a stake. Near by another stake has a fishing-line attached to it. A second line is tied to a drooping palm frond. When, toward evening, the hooks are baited, there is not long to wait, for in those waters fish are easily caught. 'C'est assez frais, ce poisson,' says Madame, as she puts one before me at my evening meal.

The hotel is not a big one. In one building there are bedrooms for half a dozen guests, in another there is a dining-room to seat the same number. Inside the dining-room, with its lattice blinds, one might be in some roadside

232

estaminet in France. There is the checkered cloth on the table, and the long rolls of crisp bread, and bowls of strong coffee, and omelettes and salads, with rough red wine to drink.

It is beside this hotel that people congregate to await the arrival of 'shipping.' It may be a launch from Papeete that arrives with mails and stores and passengers. It may be a smaller fishing-boat, heralded by the blowing of a conch shell to announce that there is fish for sale. It may be the dug-out of the Catholic priest, incongruous with its outboard motor. The launches do not stay long beside the pier; just long enough for the crew to drink a glass of beer. After they have gone the few passengers that have arrived loiter awhile to retail any news. But soon they disperse and the hotel resumes its normal calm.

A rough road circles the island, but the main traffic keeps to the water. At all times of the day canoes may be seen passing up and down or crossing the bay. Some carry fishermen and are piled with nets, some may be loaded with bananas, or coco-nuts, or bundles of firewood, or sacks of vanilla, or a pig. Many of the canoes are painted bright colours—cobalt blue, canary yellow, maroon.

One evening I saw in the distance a canoe with what seemed to be a tree on board. As it drew closer the tree resolved itself into two large coco-nut fronds, lashed together to form a sail. In the stern of the canoe sat a young man with a sleeping child on his knee. Another child lay asleep in the bottom of the canoe. The man held a steering paddle in one hand, but he made no apparent movement. Neither did the children stir. Even the frondlets of the sail did not betray the wind. On the clear, glass-like water they glided past as though enchanted.

But sometimes tragedy breaks the enchantment of the isles. A few days before I reached Cook's Bay a launch had gone tuna fishing from the neighbouring Papetoai Bay. In handling a big fish, one of the crew had lost his balance and fallen into the sea. Immediately a shark had got him, biting off his arm and cutting deep into his side. His companions, by throwing out all the fish they had on board, managed to distract the shark while they got the injured man on board. But their help was unavailing. He died that night from loss of blood.

Moorea was a stronghold of the early missionaries. It was in Afareaitu, on the eastern side of the island facing Tahiti, that they set up their printing press, and it was there that, on 30th June 1817, King Pomare under their instructions printed 'the first page of the first book published in the South Sea Islands.' The king had been sympathetic to the project from the first, and as soon as he heard that the printing office was in order he hastened to the settlement. There, with 'the composing stick in his hand, he took the capital letters, one by one out of their respective compartments, and, fixing them, concluded the alphabet.' He was then most anxious to see the page printed, and visited the press almost daily while the remainder of the first sheet was in preparation. When all was ready for printing he came, attended by two of his favourite chiefs and a numerous train of attendants, and having inked the type with his own hands he pulled the handle of the press. The paper being removed, 'the chiefs and attendants rushed towards it, to see what effect the king's pressure had produced. When they beheld the letters black, and large, and well defined, there was one simultaneous expression of wonder and delight.' From then on multitudes arrived from every district to see 'this astonishing machine.' So great was the influx of strangers that for several weeks 'the district of Afareaitu resembled a public fair.'

It was at this same period that the native women appeared 'desirous to assimilate their dresses in some degree' to that of the missionaries' wives. Hitherto, since the advent of European trade, they had worn a length of cotton either around the waist or as a 'shawl loosely covering the greater part of the body.' But now a 'garment' was designed for them. It was 'a kind of Roman tunic, usually of white or blue calico . . . fastened round the neck with a short collar, which, if possible, was united by a bright gilt or plated button. The sleeves were long and loose, and buttoned at the wrists, while the lower parts reached nearly to the ankles.' We are told that 'as the natives experienced the convenience of the new dresses, their desire for them increased, and the long loose dress soon became an everyday garment,' and 'from making plain, straightforward garments, the more expert were anxious to advance still higher; and in process of time, frills appeared round the neck; and, ultimately, caps covered the heads, and shoes and stockings clothed the feet.' Hats and bonnets soon followed, and the desire for them 'was not confined to those who possessed other articles of foreign dress, it being extended even to such as had none. Thus, wearing a hat and bonnet was the first advance they made towards a more civilized appearance and dress.'

Well! Give me 'the heathen goddesses that wore no bodices,' to quote Richard Milliken, that other great writer from Cork.

CHAPTER THIRTY-FIVE

I WAS STANDING on the waterfront at Papeete, watching a man painting the figure-head of a schooner, when a woman approached me.

'I think you are Monsieur Bob,' she said.

I looked at her for a moment. 'And I think **you** are Lili,' I replied.

'I think you are right,' she said, smiling.

We crossed the road and entered the *jardin public*.

'Dix-huit ans! Mais vous n'avez pas changé. Non! Non! Not one little bit,' she said.

'Et vous, non plus,' I said. 'La même chose exactement.'

'Un peu grisonnants,' she said, touching the thick plait of hair that crested her head.

We strolled together to a seat under a frangipane-tree. The grass was starred with fallen blossoms, ivory white.

'And Johnny?' I asked.

'Johnny is dead. Six—no, five years ago. I not married again. You remember Tom—Tom Auvergne? I live with him now. Perhaps one day we get married. Oh, but I

236

was so sad for Johnny. He was so kind. Never, never, never, not one unkind word did he say. There was not one person in all the world that did not think him his friend. But he drink too much, too much. When you know him he drink only little. But after, when his father die, he get money from home, and then he drink, drink, drink. I say to him often: "Johnny, you kill yourself, you die one day with all the drink." But he only smile at me. He alway smile at me when I scold him.'

Lili paused a moment. 'And it is eighteen years since you been here?' she said. 'Eighteen years since all that good time! You remember that picnic we had to the waterfall, with my mother and Johnny and all the girls, and my mother try teach you speak Tahitian? She still speak only very little French. I been in England since that time, that's how I learn speak English. Johnny take me to stay with his people in England. Oh, it was so nice—I *was* happy. Johnny's mother and sister they very, very kind to me, make me happy. They very good religious people, the sister she play the organ in the chapel, and they live very near to the chapel, and on Sunday they go there all the day. And they never have a drink or a smoke, and they sorry for me because they think Johnny drink and they think the drink burn up his lungs. But they never think I have a drink, so I not tell them. But sometimes I want a drink very much, and then Johnny and me go outside, up the street, and when we have our drink the boy in the bar give us a sweet, and he say then nobody know we have a drink.

'And how they all laugh at me! One day I pick a big bouquet of beautiful yellow flowers that I find, and I bring them home and I say: "Look what I find!" And they say: "What you pick those for?" I say: "But they are beautiful," and they say: "Those only buttercups, we not pick those," and then they laugh at me. And one day we go in the bush, pick bluebells. And the little child that come with us, she make a *lei* of daisies and hang it round my neck.'

Lili stooped and picked up a blossom of the frangipane that had fallen at her feet.

'When we get to England,' she continued, 'I see the trees, and they all bare, no leaf anywhere. And I say to Johnny: "How ugly they are, these trees, I think they all dead." Then of a sudden they come covered in leaves. And the may-trees all over blossom, and beautiful scent. All the trees come alive again.

'One day Johnny take me to the big garden at Kew, and then we see houses of glass, very very tall houses, and we go into them and there are beautiful mango-trees and palm-trees and bananas, just like they grow here; and I see the taro growing, and then I cry and cry because it make me homesick. Oh, the taro, it make me so homesick. And then we go out and we see the cherry-trees everywhere, all covered with flowers, white and pink, and very big high trees growing, and pools of water with flowers in them, and then I am happy again. And then we come out of the garden, and we go on to a bus and we go up into London to the Strand, and we get out of the bus and go into a Lyon hotel for some *kai*. And Johnny say to me: "You order a steak and onion for me while I go out to shipping office. Don't you move," he say, "or you get lost—I be back in two minute." So I order a steak and onion for Johnny, he alway like that, and I order some other food for me, and the girl bring the food and I sit there and wait for Johnny. Half-hour go by, hour go by, and Johnny not come back, and I sit there and I feel terrible. Oh, I feel terrible! I think perhaps Johnny in some bar, or have some accident. Very lucky for me I have some money in my bag. Johnny's overcoat for the rain is on the chair next to my seat, and I wonder if Johnny get wet. So then when two hours have pass, I pay for the two plates and I take up the coat and I go outside. I see a bus which say Victoria on it, and I get on to the bus in the queue of people, and it stop by our hotel where we stay. And I go in and all the boys come around, because they know Johnny and me, and they say: "Your husband very worried for you, he say you in Lyon hotel and he can't find which one it is, and he want us ring up all the Lyon hotel in London, but there are many hundred of them." So I say: "Where is my husband?" And they say: "He is in the room." So I go up to the room, and Johnny is there, and oh, but he is very glad to see me come, and he tell me he leave the shipping office and he cannot find the Lyon hotel where he leave me, and he look and he look, and then he come to our hotel where we stay, and there he sit and wait, and he is very frighten because he alway say to me I must never go out in London by myself because I get lost. But it was he get lost—I not get lost.

'And when it is time for us to come back to the Islands, I say to his sister: "Now I have come stay with you in England, one day you come stay with me in Islands." And she say: "Oh, I very frighten go to Islands." And I say: "But why you frighten?" She say: "I very frighten of all the cannibals and spears." And I laugh very much at that and I say: "But you not frighten with me!" And then she say: "You different, you not cannibal." And I say: "But they all just like me." But she very frighten, and I not able stop laughing because she too frighten to come.

'Then we get on the ship, and I very sorry to leave England, because every one so kind, but I am glad that Johnny see his mother and sister again. And I am very happy that we coming back to the Islands. When Johnny say he want take me to England, I not want to go. But he promise he bring me back again to the Islands, so we go. And then we come back. When we call at Bombay, it is terrible there, there are so many people—beggars, Johnny call them—lying on the road, holding up their hands to us. And I say to Johnny: "How horrible these people are; I think it is terrible to see people like that." But Johnny he say to me: "My dear Lili, you must not say that, because now you see what poorness really is. In the Islands no one is ever hungry—if he have no money there is alway taro, and he can catch plenty fish. Here they have no money and they have not anything to eat, and they are starving because they have not any food." And then I think to myself, I will alway remember what he say. And often now I think of all those people who are sad because they have not any food to eat, and here in the Islands we have so very much for every one, and so much happiness.'

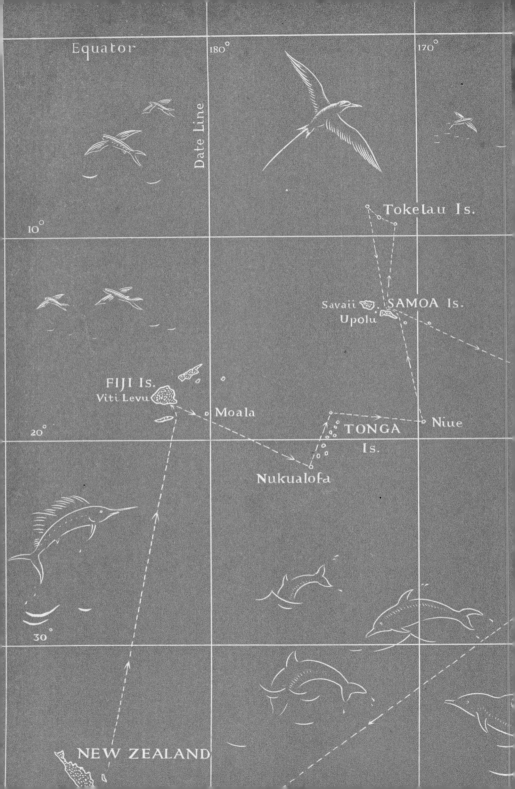